CUSTOMER SERVICE IS A CONTACT Sport™

Insight Publishing Company
Sevierville, Tennessee

CUSTOMER SERVICE IS A CONTACT Sport™

© 2003 by Performance Publishing, LLC

All rights reserved. No part of this book may be reproduced in any form or by any means without prior written permission from the author except for brief quotations embodied in critical essay, article, or review. These articles and/or reviews must state the correct title, author and publisher of this book by name.

Published by Insight Publishing Company
P.O. Box 4189
Sevierville, Tennessee 37864

Cover Design & Book Layout by Russ Hollingsworth
Edited by Mitch Moore

Printed in the United States of America

ISBN 1-885640-95-1

Table Of Contents

Acknowledgements iv
About The Author v
Introduction vii

Chapter One
Customer Service Is A Contact Sport™ 9

Chapter Two
Great Customer Service Starts With A Vision 19

Chapter Three
The Service Experience 25

Chapter Four
Employees With The Right Service Attitude 33

Chapter Five
Facility Imaging And Merchandising 63

Chapter Six
The Systems Behind Great Customer Service 79

Chapter Seven
Maximizing Revenue Per Customer 91

Chapter Eight
Complaints—A Gift From Your Customer 101

Chapter Nine
Measurement And Management 115

A Personal Note 126

ACKNOWLEDGEMENTS

First, I thank God for His blessings and gifts that enrich my life and enable me beyond my own capabilities.

To my wife, Terri, whose love is the inspiration that motivates me and whose support and positive attitude make every day special. Your smile lights my day—you are truly the woman of my dreams.

To my son, Taylor, who from the day he was born has inspired me to become a better person and the father I am proud to be. You help me keep everything in its proper perspective.

And to all the other people in my life who see my visions and encourage me to live my dreams—thank you.

You all make my life what it is every day.

About The Author

Joseph Rosales is the founder and president of Customer Service Solutions, Inc., a consulting and training firm that specializes in helping companies develop the people, processes and systems that enable them to consistently achieve customer service excellence.

A native of southern California, Joseph began his retail career in 1972, working in the men's clothing industry and learning great customer service techniques from his first retail managers—Angelo Scorsone, Ron Brown and Michael Pallan. Joseph credits his early experience as being one of the strongest influences on his customer service perspectives today.

Showing early success at sales and managing people, Joseph was promoted to department manager within a year. Over the next fifteen years, he continued to develop his management and retailing skills in men's clothing and, later, in the fine jewelry industry.

In 1987, Joseph moved to Seattle, Washington, where he met his wife, Terri. He lived several years in the Northwest, eventually trying his hand at marketing residential and commercial real estate. While earning and learning opportunities were plentiful, Joseph's heart was still focused on the retail service industry.

Joseph and Terri eventually moved to Colorado to be closer to the world-class skiing the area offered. Soon, however, Joseph was recruited as a director of operations by a franchisor of automotive service facilities. He was able to apply his retailing and customer service skills to an industry that, at the time, was nearly devoid of good customer service models.

Today, through his position as president of Customer Service Solutions, Inc., Joseph has the opportunity to work with some of the largest retailing organizations, yet he still stays in touch with the smaller businesses that make up so much of retailing today.

Joseph is a frequent speaker at national conventions and sales meetings and writes extensively on customer service. His straightforward and highly effective models for developing and delivering excellent customer service are used by some of the most successful retailers around the world.

Introduction

Excellent customer service is the lifeblood of virtually every service-oriented business. Whether you run a restaurant, bank, clothing store, automotive service center or grocery market, customer service is the most definable way to separate your business from the competition. Unfortunately, customer service excellence is quickly becoming a lost expectation in retail businesses.

It isn't because retailers don't agree that great service is an important element of a service experience and an important component of the value a customer receives; they do. But providing excellent customer service requires more of an effort—an effort most business owners are not willing to make. However, one can easily demonstrate that providing excellent customer service actually takes less time and provides both immediate and positive, long-term results.

Consistently providing excellent customer service will not only increase sales, improve customer loyalty and reduce customer complaints but also improve employee performance and retention. And you will enjoy your business more. After all, personal fulfillment and enjoyment are among the fundamental reasons one chooses any career.

This book is written mostly for people who own, operate, manage or have an interest in successful retail businesses. However, anyone in a business that serves customers will benefit from the suggestions and ideas contained in this book.

By definition, a retail business is any business where a customer goes to purchase a product or service and is served by an employee. Even with the advent of the Internet, being a customer of a retail business is still an everyday occurrence to all of us. In the process of running normal errands—getting gas for your car, picking up bread at the store or picking up your dry cleaning—you will come in contact with an employee who can add to your experience in a positive or negative way and therefore affect the value of the product or service you are purchasing. There is no escaping the impact that customer service has on the success of a business. In my mind, the greatest challenge to successful retailers is to provide excellent customer service, every day and with every customer.

Much like a professional sports team, a successful retail organization needs to acquire the best players, help them develop the highest skills and develop a solid game strategy. And to bring it all together, the team must have a good coach who is capable of bringing out the best in his players.

Throughout this book, we will examine how excellent customer service can be attained and maintained in your business, not just occasionally or with only a few special customers you know and like, but every day and with every customer. By the end of this book, you will come to understand why I say, "Customer Service Is A Contact Sport." (TM)

Chapter One

Customer Service Is A Contact Sport™

Every contact with every customer makes a difference in the ultimate success of your business.

I find it interesting how difficult customer service is to define. In fact, it changes from customer to customer and from day to day. For example, if I am in your store today, and I am in a hurry for some reason, time is of the essence if I am to perceive great customer service. However, if I am in your store tomorrow, and I am not in a hurry, then time is less important to me. Although time is almost always an issue in the customer service equation, it is only one of several components that will need to be addressed in your quest to provide world-class customer service.

The concept that customer service is a contact sport can be evidenced in many different ways, from a welcoming smile to a friendly handshake or a sincere "thank you." Virtually every contact you have with a customer creates an impression and a subsequent value for him or her. After all, people do business with people, and they do more business with people they like. Other businesses may offer similar products or services, often at a reduced price, but great service isn't always part of what you receive.

Even more unfortunate is the fact that many of us as customers are learning to accept an ever-declining level of customer service. We are, in essence, becoming customer service desensitized. Many people tell us they are less inclined to complain when they receive poor service because they just don't have the time. And incidences of poor service are more numerous than ever before, which raises one of the most concerning issues of all—that the majority of customers will not tell you when you have failed to meet their expectations; they will just quietly decide not to return to your business. Consider the customer's perspective. Why should they take the time to tell you that you did not meet their expectations or even provide good service? If you truly cared, you wouldn't have let it happen in the first place. So be aware: you may not be receiving customer complaints because many customers vote with their feet.

Generally, most people will say good customer service is simply meeting the customer's needs. Pretend for a moment that you own a jewelry store. A customer comes in for a watch battery; you have it, they purchase it, and they leave. Using that measurement, was good customer service achieved? If you are already in a customer service business, then you recognize how many other opportunities there were in that one transaction to deliver great customer service—from offering to install the battery, to cleaning the customer's jewelry, to offering her a complimentary cup of coffee or a ring inspection. There are many ways, even with the most basic of transactions, to raise the bar on customer service delivery.

Oftentimes, winning a customer's repeat business is *not* based entirely on the quality of the product purchased or the convenience of the service provided, although meeting those needs is, of course, a prerequisite to great customer service.

Customer Service Is A Contact Sport™

Customers rightfully expect a product will meet their needs, but when you impress them with great service, you establish a standard most other businesses will rarely attain. Great customer service should be a foundational aspect of your business model, and every member of your staff should understand that he or she is responsible for developing and maintaining customer relationships. Remember, the most productive use of your time related to business development is making contact and talking to your customers.

Let me give you one quick example of how good customer contact makes a difference in the value of a shopping experience. Recently, while I was out of town on business, I was shopping in an office supply store and asked an employee where I might find a certain item. Instead of simply telling me the aisle number and pointing in the general direction of the item, he promptly walked me to its precise location and, after asking me a few qualifying questions, assisted me in selecting the best item for my purpose. Once my selection was made, he then asked what other items I might be looking for. Since I needed nothing else, he told me that he would check me out if I was ready. He was more than courteous and made it a point to make me feel as though he was interested in me as a customer, conversing with me in a casual and respectful manner.

When I learned from his name tag that he was the store manager, I commented on how impressed I was that he would take the time to help me personally instead of calling for one of his employees take care of me. His response was consistent with his customer service demeanor: "I would rather be on the sales floor making contact with customers, having fun and assuring everyone is being properly taken care of than be in the office doing paperwork. I can have others do the paperwork; my job is assuring that customer service is our highest priority." Now this is a manager who understands the importance of customer service and of being a positive example to his employees. If I lived in that area, I would go out of my way to shop at this business.

It is vital that your staff understands the importance of excellent customer service and that everyone is committed to delivering exceptional customer service every day. To do that, you must be an example to your staff and demonstrate what exceptional customer service looks like.

The Importance Of Contact

Each and every contact you make with a customer matters, but it takes more than just a smile and a "thank you" to ensure good customer service. To be sure, being nice is more than just not being rude. I often see people give the most basic customer responses, and although they are not being rude, they are barely being nice. It's something I call "sterile efficiency."

Being attended to by someone who does not appear to like you or openly dislikes his or her job is not going to project a friendly attitude. Have you ever been served by this type of individual? Have you ever inquired about how he or she is doing that day and gotten a response similar to: "I'll be better in about fifteen minutes when my shift is over." That response can only tell a customer that the employee does not like his job or that he would rather not be waiting on this, or any, customer. Neither is a good impression. A more appropriate response to this inquiry would be to say, "I'm doing great. Thank you for asking," or "I'm fine. How are you?" The answer should make the customer feel good about asking the question.

Making your customers feel cared for in an individualized way can significantly enhance the value of the service you provide. Every contact made with a customer is an opportunity for you to learn just how his or her particular needs can be met.

Here is another example of how good service will lead to satisfied customers and revenue for your business. When it was time to upgrade our home audio and video system to the newest DVD and digital audio components, I decided to go shopping. I had no knowledge of the technology that was available, so I shopped three different stores to familiarize myself with the options.

At the first store, I had to track down someone to answer my questions, finally finding a young man who said he could help me. I proceeded to tell him that I was interested in purchasing a complete home entertainment system. Without even asking me about my preferences and without any effort to get a perspective on my personal knowledge, he began to show me some low-end systems that were on sale. After letting him show me all of his closeout models, I finally interrupted and told him that I was really looking to purchase a high-end system and that money was not my first consideration. He seemed put off by my request to show me the higher-end systems. When he did, it seemed as though we rushed through the performance issues, and he quickly brought me back to the sale systems. Not finding him supportive of my needs, I left the store and continued shopping.

Upon entering the audio department of the next store, I saw two young men engaged in conversation. I approached and stood a few feet away from them for awhile before they finally stopped talking to each other. One of them asked me, "What do you need?" I said I needed someone to sell me a home entertainment system. The young man said he could help me and led me over to their display of systems, asking me no questions about what I needed. As I listened to what he told me about the products, I kept getting the feeling that he was more interested in impressing me with his knowledge and less interested in helping me pick a system that was right for me. After awhile, I thanked him and told him I appreciated his time and that I would ask for him if I decided to buy from his store.

When I entered the audio department of the third store, I noticed a man doing what looked like inventory work. I asked him if he knew about home entertainment systems, and he replied that he was one of the senior consultants in the department and that he had a passion for audio equipment; he even joked that he may even bore me with too much information. We both laughed, and he asked me a few questions about what kind of audio/video system I currently had, my general plans for how I would use the new system and what budget he should keep in mind. We spoke for several minutes before he began demonstrating some of the products. He told me about the features of each one and how the systems differed from each other, occasionally referring back to my objectives. After about thirty minutes of demonstration, I told him that I would like to buy a system from him, and I asked him which one he would recommend. He told me, and I bought it on the spot. Price was never an issue, as is often the case with many customers. I got great service from a knowledgeable person who took the time to inform me of my options and made it easy for me to buy a system. Sincere service that was specific to my personal audio/video needs led to a big sale.

Through our consulting company, we have innumerable opportunities to see what is being done both successfully and unsuccessfully in businesses across the country. Quite literally, there may be a dozen businesses in one market that are providing the same basic products or services, but in most cases, only a few of them will be doing the lion's share of the business. The companies may have the same name-brand products, the same type of equipment and the same pricing structure, but one business will have a line of customers while another business down the street will be empty.

We all know that when one provider is more successful than another, it usually involves some element of customer service and perceived value. But how does the successful business achieve this dominance in the customer service game? What is the secret? I believe the answer has less to do with secrets than with retailing basics. These basics, or keys, are hidden to many business operators yet can be revealed by identifying what are commonly called best practices.

Best Practice

The concept of best practice is by no means new to business; in fact, many of you may already employ this concept in your business. For those of you who are not familiar with the best practice concept, it means seeking out the best and most effective way of doing something and then doing it that way. As anyone who plays golf knows, it is not the good shots that you have to improve—it is the shots that don't go where they are supposed to go. If your weakness is putting, then working on that aspect of your game will improve your scores. Likewise, if you generally deliver a good product but customer relationship building is an area in which you could improve, then start working on it—and the sooner the better. On the surface, this sounds simple—and it is in some respects—but few businesses even bother to seek out best practices.

I strongly believe that if there is a way to do something, there is a best way and a worst way. Take something as basic as your customer greeting. There are many ways to greet and introduce a new customer to your business. They can range from a friendly "hello" or an introduction to a barely audible grunt, a head nod or "How can I help you?" Some greetings are more effective than others and will convey a different impression to your customer. If you are truly committed to improving the overall performance of your business, then you should constantly seek out those best ways and make them your standards. After all, don't your employees and customers deserve the best you are capable of?

Optimize Your Business

No business is perfect, and no system is perfect; nor is it realistic to assume either one could be. However, it is possible to achieve optimal levels of service—not *perfect* service but the best results you can achieve given the resources, skills and talent you have available. Look closely at your business. What do you think could be improved? Don't be limited by your own past experience with your business. It never ceases to amaze me how a fresh perspective can often raise the performance of a company to higher levels than anyone previously thought possible.

Regardless of what your business is, there's always a way to optimize. For example, I race slot cars as a hobby. Many of you may remember them from the late '60s and '70s—little model cars powered by small electric motors. Today, some divisions of these cars are capable of speeds exceeding 100 miles per hour (yes, real miles per hour). I love preparing and racing these scale replicas of real cars, and I am fortunate to win or place in the top three at most races I enter. Other racers often ask me, "We are using the same chassis, body and motor components. Why is your car so much faster than mine?" or "How do you get your cars to handle so well?" Unfortunately (or fortunately, depending on your perspective!), the answer is never a simple one because there isn't just one factor at play. If there are thirty choices, adjustments, setups and preparations I can do to make a car go fast and handle well, and if I do all thirty of them well, then I will most likely have a faster car than the others who only made a few of the enhancements or didn't do them all that well.

Look at NASCAR racing today. Every one of the forty-three cars on the track basically has the same components and the same number of people on the team. So why are some teams and cars faster week in and week out? The answer has a lot to do with the fact that the teams running in the front of the pack are simply doing more things right and giving themselves more opportunity to win. Sure, getting a good break always helps, but if there is a best setup for that car, at that track, on that day, the winning teams will figure it out. If there is a best way to change four tires, fill a gas tank, clean a windshield and get it all done in less than fourteen seconds, the winning teams will find a way to get it done every week.

Likewise, if there are thirty things you can do to make your business more successful, then the more of them you do and the more effectively you do them, the more successful your business will become. Today, right now—take a look around you. Are you optimized, maximized and energized, or are you just doing the basics and merely selling products and processing transactions?

Customer Service Is A Contact Sport™

Chapter One Summary
- Every customer contact matters.
- Customers are where the action is.
- Apply best practices to your business.
- Optimize your business.

Chapter Two

Great Customer Service Starts With A Vision

> **You are the visionary and the artist. You design the experience and control how the service is delivered and perceived by your customer.**

How would you visualize your business—and your customer service in particular—if you were not encumbered by the paradigms that limit you? If you could literally snap your fingers and have a perfect business, perfect employees giving perfect customer service and even perfect customers who appreciate your commitment to service excellence, what would that vision look like? Does it seem like a dream? Well, that dream *should* be the vision for your business.

I am blessed to have the opportunity to meet with hundreds of business owners every year to discuss their business challenges. The most requested focus of nearly every consulting project we perform is helping a client improve some aspect of customer service. Everyone talks about providing excellent customer service, yet most people we talk to have a difficult time even trying to define customer service. In other words, they find it difficult to define their vision for customer service. To some, customer service just means being friendly; to others, it is providing a superior product or doing a technically correct job.

While these statements are important elements of good service, they are merely components of an excellent customer service experience and by themselves do not constitute excellent service.

Think about it. Have you ever been a customer at a business where the people were very nice but failed to meet your base expectations for why you went to their business in the first place? Conversely, have you ever been to a business where got what you wanted but it seemed the people couldn't have cared less that you were there? For excellent customer service to happen, you need to deliver both components—friendly caring service *and* delivery of the product or service.

What motivates a customer to go to a business—the cheapest price, the largest selection, the fastest service or something entirely different? Indeed, there are many other values to your retailing model that create benefits for your customer. However, if your customers like you, then issues like price, selection and speed take a secondary position in the value equation. I am not suggesting that basic values like price, quality and convenience are not important, but they are easier to meet and surpass by the competition. If you have ever lowered your prices only to see that price reduction met by a competitor, you have experienced the effect of trying to attract and keep customers based on price alone. And remember that the lower your price, the less profit you make.

Some business models do very well attracting customers with competitive pricing. Take Wal-Mart, for example. They promote themselves as having the lowest prices and on many items achieve that goal. That's because everything Wal-Mart does supports the low price initiative, from their ordering and inventory systems to their physical stores and, ultimately, their employees. Even though they are constantly pressing the low price envelope, they are reasonably successful at producing acceptable and, in many cases, exceptional customer service. But remember that Wal-Mart is mostly a self-serve business. The less self-serve your business is, the more that engaging, personalized customer service figures into the total value equation for the customer.

So how do you go about establishing a vision that will create not just satisfied customers but ones who are completely committed to your business and will go out of their way to be so? Let's start with some basic yet time-tested ideas:

First, decide how you want your service to be perceived. Don't limit yourself to how service is currently provided at your business or by how your competitors provide it. Just decide in the limitless world of your imagination what a perfect customer service experience would be like. How would your staff greet the customer? What would they say to make this customer feel special? How will they be dressed? How will your employees be groomed? How will they identify the customer's wants or needs? How will they explain your product or service? What would your environment look like, and how would it feel to the customer? Nearly everything that affects a customer service experience is within your control. You are the visionary and the artist. You control how the picture is delivered and perceived by your customer.

Second, be sure what your customer wants. This may sound obvious, but from our interviews with operators of many different types of businesses, we have found that most have never asked their customers what they want. It is an erroneous and dangerous assumption to assume that every customer wants the same things and that they want them provided in the same way.

Years ago, when I was in the jewelry business, I was completely underwhelmed at how so many of the beautiful rings I would place in the display cases would not sell! I was positive I had great taste in jewelry and thought that if my customers could just see the rings through my eyes, they would surely buy them. But I had to count that as another lesson learned: everyone doesn't like what I like. Some customers like the big, gaudy rings and the heavy gold chains that I would never wear. It quickly became apparent that my job was not to change my customers' tastes or make them accept what I liked but to continuously become aware of what they liked and do my best to have that in stock.

Finding out what your customers want is going to take some time and effort; however, it will definitely be worth it. Start by talking to your customers. Ask what is important to them, and listen carefully to what they say. Not only will you get some good ideas but you will be showing your customers that their input and suggestions are important to you. (We'll discuss customer research tools such as surveys and questionnaires later in the book.)

Third, exceed your customer's expectations. What the customer wants should be your *minimum* standard. If she wants quick service, make it obviously quick. If she wants friendly service then make sure every service contact is friendly and engaging. Make it obvious that your people are friendly and that you are going the extra mile. A smile, a nod of the head, a handshake, a sincere goodbye—any of these can let a customer know you are attentive and that you're there to care about her needs. Making a goal of exceeding expectations will not only result in more customers dedicated to your service but in a more enjoyable service experience for you and your employees.

If all of this seems a bit exacting to you, consider what makes a superstar in any business, sport or profession; it is a commitment to become the best. That commitment takes vision, planning and a lot of work. If you want to be the best, it may involve doing some things differently than you do today.

All retail businesses are built around the same basic premise—provide a product or service to customers in a way that makes them want to return again and again. Consistently providing excellent customer service is more process than art. Most anyone with the desire and ability to visualize, organize and communicate that vision to others can accomplish what some feel is impossible—delivering excellent service to virtually every customer.

Chapter Two Summary

- Visualize the perfect customer service experience.
- Remember what motivates your customers.
- How do you want your customer service to be perceived?
- Make sure you know what your customer wants.
- Exceed your customer's expectations.

Customer Service Is A Contact Sport™

Chapter Three

The Service Experience

Customers remember how they were treated long after they have used the product or consumed the service.

Is Your Service Memorable?

When working with a client we often find that even if they are generally nice to their customers, they still do little to develop relationships with these very people who fund their business. Thus, business owners often find that their customer unit counts are not growing, and even while new services or products are being added, the revenues generated do not make up for the decline in customers.

Don't forget that for most people, shopping rates right up there with going to the dentist or having their taxes done, and simply providing a quality product or technically correct service will do only so much to guarantee that a customer will go out of his way to return to your business. What customers most often remember about any service experience is how the people who served them made them feel. Making a service experience more memorable (positively, not negatively) can be easier and more fun for both you and the customer, and it pays big dividends in helping you expand your customer base.

There are many ways to make people feel comfortable at your business. It may be as simple as addressing a return visitor by name or introducing yourself to a new customer. Obviously there is a fine line between gabbing someone into a state of boredom and communicating information that can be productive, so properly training your staff and monitoring the process is important.

The physical condition of your business plays a role as well. Are your restrooms not only spotless but appropriately decorated? We all know from personal experience the impression that a dirty restroom can make. For virtually all of your customers, especially your female customers, clean, well-decorated restrooms rank high on the list of things that will make a favorable impression.

Great Service is More Than Just Not Being Mean

I would like to expand on this concept that I introduced in Chapter One. In nearly every type of business, we experience people who are just going through the motions and activities that make up their jobs. They do their jobs and provide the services, but they don't do anything to make customers feel that they really care or that it matters to them if the customers are happy with the service they are receiving.

To illustrate this point, I'll share a recent incident. During lunch with a client in New Orleans, I casually asked our waitress how she was doing. Her reply was, "Not very well today, but I'm here." I thought, "Now that is an interesting way to make a customer feel welcome." When I replied, "Sorry you are having a bad day," she proceeded to mention that she is looking for a new job and can't wait to find a one. As we observed her "taking care of her other customers," it became obvious that she knew the menu and was proficient at taking care of the customers' basic needs, but that was about the extent of her involvement.

Although she was not mean to anyone that I observed, it was obvious that she was not making an effort to make any friends or win customers.

Unfortunately, this is usually the standard of service many of us receive. The product focus is there, but a focus on the customer is secondary. And ironically, the customer is the decision maker and will eventually decide if he or she will return for service. That being said, it makes sense that our customers should be one of the highest priorities.

Taking time to develop a customer relationship is one of the most underutilized business-building skills I see in every segment of retail. Yes, I do see many businesses doing a great job of caring for and developing their customers, but it is far less of an occurrence than it should be. Making customers happy is a much different objective than just not making them mad.

The Moment of Truth

While reading a book about the founder of Scandinavian Airlines a few years ago, I was struck by the concept of "the moment of truth." The moment of truth illustrates the dynamics that make up a typical customer experience and result in a decision on whether a customer will return to a particular business—or, in this case, fly on Scandinavian Airlines.

Your business may not be carrying passengers on airplanes, but every customer makes a decision to come back to your business based on a specific occurrence or group of occurrences during his or her service experience. While consulting with hundreds of business owners every year, I have come to appreciate this simple reality—the moment of truth. Often it is not one single issue that wins a customer over or drives them to the competition; more often, just a few little things done right will cause a customer to make the decision to return to your business.

Here is a scenario that you might have experienced:

You have decided to try out a new restaurant you have passed on many occasions. You walk into the restaurant, and within a few moments, a friendly person greets and welcomes you. This person is smiling and genuinely seems glad to see you. While seating you, she tells you that your server, Jim, will be with you in a few moments. As you and your guest look around, you notice how well-decorated the restaurant is and how everything seems so orderly. Soon Jim comes to the table, welcomes you, introduces himself and offers to take your drink order. He compliments your guest on her choice of drink. Shortly, he returns with your drinks and presents them to you with a bit of flair, not just tossing them on the table. He invites you to try the drinks and make sure they are to your liking.

Jim gives you more time with menu, and when he comes back, he recites the specials with clarity and passion. He notices your indecision and takes time to ask what kind of food you feel like eating that night—fish, chicken or meat. He makes some personal suggestions, which you appreciate. After you and your guest order, Jim heads for the kitchen, reminding you to let him know if you need anything at all.

Within a few moments, another server, Sarah, comes by and says she will be assisting Jim. She brings you warm sourdough bread with butter. She fills your glasses and asks if everything is satisfactory. You notice how well Jim and Sarah work as a team. They are engaging and friendly without being intrusive, and they appear to be enjoying their jobs.

The Service Experience

This is an ideal experience, but there are plenty of opportunities for the moment of truth to rear its head. The waiter could wait too long to take your order. After sitting for fifteen or twenty minutes without being able to flag down another waiter, you may get up and decide never to return to the restaurant as a result of the poor service. The food could be overcooked or too cold. It could be poorly prepared or just not taste good. The waiter could disappear on his break or make you wait forever for your check. The non-smoking section could have a smoker in it, or Jim and Sarah could forget to check on you or clear your plates from the table. These are just a few of the things that could go wrong. And while the moment of truth most often happens near the end of the service experience, any of these incidents could contribute to the moment of truth—that moment when a person decides whether or not to go back to an establishment.

Are you actively seeking the best way to do things within your business? Are you consistently providing training and support for your employees so that they will provide an excellent service experience? Remember, you can't escape the moment of truth. You can, however, make sure that every customer has a positive experience from beginning to end, which will lead to the moment of truth being in your favor.

What Are Your Customer Service Standards?

A few years ago, I had the opportunity to be the keynote speaker at a client's convention in Hawaii. My topic was creating a customer service culture in a service business. During the session, I covered the key points of creating a culture in one's business wherein excellence in customer service is the standard. There are, in fact, three critical components to delivering

Customer Service Is A Contact Sport™

exceptional customer service. Many other factors contribute to this as well, but these three components, or competencies, are the most important activities businesses should focus on to create an environment that fosters great customer service.

The first component is the people who work in your business and serve your customers. (In a later chapter of this book, we will cover some of the basics of how to effectively recruit, train, develop and motivate the employees who serve your customers.) The second component is the facility, the place your customers go to purchase your products and services, and the third component is the systems and processes that create the service experience your customers will receive.

This is really where the magic of customer service happens. They may sound basic and common sense, but these components are critical to establishing an environment that produces happy customers. And it has been my personal experience, in interviewing thousands of operators of service businesses, that rarely are all three areas handled simultaneously.

At best, one may find an operator who has one or two of the three components dialed in. During an initial business consultation, I was speaking to a gentleman who runs a successful chain of retail stores. We started talking on the subject of hiring employees, and I was challenged by some of his comments. He felt that it was nearly impossible to hire good people in his industry. He explained to me the problems of not being able to offer stable hours because of the nature of his business and that he couldn't pay top dollar to his employees.

Unfortunately, I had heard this many times before, and while these things contribute to the challenge, they do not escalate the challenge to the level of impossibility. It will likely require that this gentleman may be a little more creative and proactive in finding solutions. Yes, competition for employees is tougher today than it was five or ten years ago; and competition for customers is also more demanding. There are more businesses offering more to their customers than ever before. It seems everyone offers expanded menus, super sizing and expanded product lines. Even traditional competitors are combining resources to meet the needs of an ever more demanding customer. It is not unusual to see non-traditional services offered under the same roof—a donut shop combined with an ice cream shop, a tire store combined with a coffee shop, a convenience store within a dry cleaner's. Offering your customer an expanded line of products and services increases the convenience for your customer and therefore increases your value as a provider. Customers can get more in one place and not have to seek out another unknown relationship with another business.

Remember, however, that just offering more to your customer is not the entire answer. To be the dominant provider in your marketplace requires that you excel at providing your customers with a level of service and care that they cannot get anywhere else at any price.

Don't Be Lulled Into Complacency

Many businesses feel they are doing better at maintaining a high percentage of return customers than they actually are. Only tracking return customer percentages may not tell an accurate story. For example, if you are tracking a return customer rate of seventy-five percent, that may sound good on the surface. However, if retaining seventy-five out of 100 customers is an acceptable number to your business (I personally prefer something closer to ninety percent), then you have accomplished

Customer Service Is A Contact Sport™

a worthy objective. But ask yourself why you are losing twenty-five percent of your customers. You may need to dig deeper and find out why they are not coming back. Likewise, if you are not getting a particular customer's full volume of business, then you have a great opportunity to increase revenues with that existing customer. Yes, some customers shop other places because they want a some variety, but when the experience is right, they will come to you most often.

Making your service more memorable to your customers takes some thought, and it may even cost money to upgrade some aspects of your business. But if you make the right impact on your customers, it will return your investment of time and money many times over.

Chapter Three Summary
- Make your service memorable.
- Remember the moment of truth.
- Have high customer service expectations.
- Think people, facilities and processes.
- Don't be complacent.

Chapter Four

Employees With The Right Service Attitude

> People do business with people, and they usually do more business with people they like.

In today's competitive retail marketplace, product selection, quality and merchandising have become major influences and strongly relate to how companies go to market and how consumers view value. For a retailer to achieve above-average sales in a highly saturated environment, it must rely on more than product and selection; those are the relatively easy components to duplicate in a business model. They must also rely on high levels of individualized customer service.

The factor that most affects the ability of a business to deliver a high level of customer service is the people who work with the customers. And much of the battle is won, or lost, in the selection, training and development of the employees.

The statement, "It is impossible to find good employees" has been repeated countless times, for hundreds of years and in virtually every language and country in the world. However, there have always been and always will be those people who want to deliver great customer service. As much as everything changes in our high-tech world, some things stay the same—people are our number one challenge and our greatest asset.

Maybe you suffer the same frustration shared by millions of business owners—feeling they can't get their people to do the things that will have a positive effect on their business. I mean simple things like greeting every customer with a smile and striking up a conversation instead of looking bored and just saying, "Can I help you?" Often, an employee may just sit and wait for the arrival of the next customer and, when one does come into the store, do little to develop a relationships that could increase the value of the products and services the business offers. Sound familiar?

The answer to this common challenge is more involved than just firing everyone and starting over with new employees. After all, that doesn't solve the problem; it just trades current known problems for new, unknown ones. Often, the problem of poor employee performance is rooted in the hiring of the wrong people with the wrong attitude, a lack of an effective training program, a poorly designed customer service system and, to a large degree, management's willingness to accept a low level of performance from the employees and the business.

So who are these people who will engage your customers with a friendly smile and bring life to your customer service system? Where do you find them? How do you make the time to look for them? And once found, how do you interview them to make sure they are going to be good employees? How do you motivate and inspire your retail team?

The Search Is On

One of the first steps to building a world-class customer service team is being open to the idea that you can still find highly customer service-oriented employees. Every day, I see employees at various businesses in communities across the

Employees With The Right Service Attitude

country serving customers with excellence and having a great time doing it.

My clients often feel they cannot pay enough to get quality employees and still maintain their profit margins. While not paying a competitive wage can certainly limit the available selection of the highest quality employees, the fact is that many of us have worked at jobs early in our careers for minimum wage and did a great job while we were at it. You must look for those kinds of people—people like us when we were at that point in our careers. To be sure, most motivated people will do a good job because it is the right thing to do.

However, I believe the problem stems from more than just a lack of available, quality employees. I also believe that many business owners have given up looking. They have had enough let-downs or rejections—too many negative experiences setting their sights on a higher level employee, only to be disappointed. If you are in retail, you will have to guard yourself against becoming tainted by your past experiences. Believe there are still people who will come to work with you and share your vision for customer service excellence.

As good as your customer systems can be, the truth is that all good service programs succeed because there are competent employees in place to make them succeed. There are no shortcuts, and there are no alternatives.

Let's start by looking at one of the most important character traits of the good customer service representative. Sure, they must be friendly and have that certain something that makes it a pleasure to be around them. They come in all shapes and sizes and colors, but they have one thing in common—a smile.

As I visit clients in various parts of the world, I am always reminded that no matter what language one speaks, a smile is universal and is a quiet yet powerful expression that communicates friendliness. A friendly smile is a simple but effective way to show a customer that you are glad she came to your facility. Often we find that employees and managers who come in contact with customers are not aware of how much impact their facial expressions have on a customer's initial impression of the business and how that first impression affects the rest of the experience. Customers can't read your mind, but they can read a smile. Some of the best things about smiles are:

- Smiles are free
- Smiles don't take any extra time
- You have an unlimited supply of smiles
- When you give a smile, you usually get one in return
- Smiles make both the giver and the receiver feel good

So why would people not smile at their customers? Why would someone not be friendly to a customer who is making a choice to come to a business that contributes to that employee's living? I'm sure there are many reasons and excuses, but all of them are inapplicable when you consider that a customer isn't coming to your business to feel less than welcome, to be exposed to a tale of woe or to experience a negative attitude from someone with whom she is trying to do business.

Profiling

To find the best person to serve your customers, you should start with the vision process we spoke of earlier in this book. Before you go out and begin recruiting, you must have a clear idea of what type of employee you want.

Begin your recruitment process by building a profile of your ideal employee. What are the traits you'd like to see in an employee: good grooming, clear speech, a positive attitude? Those are key qualities that you should include in your employee recruitment profile. Choose employees with team-building qualities, who will add to your customer service value.

One golden rule to follow is: Hire attitude, train competence. Different positions require different skill sets, but the single trait shared by all successful employees is a good attitude. You can teach almost anyone with a friendly demeanor to follow the service procedures that will result in a good service experience, but it is difficult, if not impossible, to teach someone how to have the right attitude.

To be sure, some positions require job-specific skills. For example, an effective manager must posses good leadership, communication and people skills. Service attendants need to be friendly and courteous as well as have the ability to work quickly and efficiently. If your business is more technical, then your candidates must possess, or you must be willing to teach them, the skills they need to deliver the services to your customers.

To help us illustrate the point, just imagine that you are responsible for recruiting players for a professional sports team. Your goal: go all the way to the championship game and win it! What kinds of players would you want on your team? If your game were basketball you would want players who could shoot, dribble, play defense and, in the end, score more points than the competition. You would also want players who play well together, can follow your game plan and who are dedicated to winning. These same elements are important to virtually any successful business. What kinds of players do you want on your world-class customer service team? What is your profile? Can anybody off the street with a pulse be on your team, or do you have higher standards?

As you develop a profile of your ideal employee, you will begin to notice those characteristics in employees working at other businesses. Writing out the character traits and skills you are looking for will establish the foundation for recruiting the best employees to serve your customers and to be valuable assets to your business.

Recruiting

The job of recruiting for a successful team is very different than coaching. Before you can begin the process of developing and practicing everything that will need to happen on game day, you first need to acquire the players.

With the profile of your ideal employee developed, you are ready to start searching for these high quality candidates. Where will you look? Remember that most of the best employees are already working somewhere else. Occasionally, ideal candidates might walk in off the street or answer an ad from the newspaper, but for the most part, they are already working and will not likely stumble across your available position.

Because you are seeking people with retail skills, who are most likely working in retail already, you have the luxury of observing them demonstrate certain characteristics while they are serving customers in their current jobs. Pay special notice to people who serve you at other businesses. You may find employee candidates at the local convenience store, hardware store, garden shop or fast food restaurant. Regardless of the size of your marketplace, you have more than enough people working in other businesses within a five- to ten-mile radius of you business to fill your openings.

Once you identify a good candidate, compliment him on a job well done, and tell him you are always looking for good people who give great customer service. Ask him if he knows anyone interested in working for a company that will appreciate a job well done, and invite them to call. If it is the right person at the right time, he will call. If he isn't interested, he may know someone who is; friendly, successful people most often hang around with people like themselves. But don't make any further contact at this point as it can be considered stealing an employee. You don't want to become known in your market as someone who is always trying to take other businesses' employees away. The seed you plant will be enough to let someone know you are looking and may harvest a good candidate in the future.

A comprehensive recruiting program should include properly designed advertisements and in-store signage and should include a referral program that compensates your current employees when they refer good candidates to you. There are many ways to set up such a program, but one of the most important elements is discussing in detail with your current employees the kinds of candidates you are looking for in advance. This will help bring the right candidates to your team and will also reinforce to your current employees the characteristics that you expect in them.

Interviewing

Once you have identified a friendly, enthusiastic customer service person in whom you are interested, it is time for the interview process—with emphasis on the word "process." An effective interview should be a series of communications opportunities between you and the candidate that will provide you with the information you need to know to decide whether or not you would like to offer that person a job.

Customer Service Is A Contact Sport™

Before we go any further, you need to make a promise—a promise that is paramount to assuring that you will be successful in hiring the right people to be on you team. The promise is: never, ever hire a candidate on the first interview. Never! You can't possibly know enough information about the candidate after just one interview. Invest the time now, or pay the price of hiring the wrong people later. The choice is yours.

A few notes before we get into the details of interviewing:

Interviewing is an important process that should be planned and practiced with the people who are going to be conducting them. There is much to be attended to: knowing and understanding how to set up the interview environment, what questions to ask and not to ask, how to phrase questions, how not to coach answers and how to properly end an interview.

To help our clients conduct more effective interviews, we developed a process we call the three-part interview. It typically is done over a period of a few days, although it can be done more quickly if extenuating circumstances exist.

This process will vary slightly, depending on how the candidate has come to know about your employment opportunity. For example, if you know the candidate already, or if she has been part of an ongoing recruitment process, then the introduction prior to the first interview would be more informal. However, if the candidate is just filling out an application, and you do not know her, you may want to schedule the first interview for another day and spend a bit more time on introductions in the first interview.

In any case, remember that this is a process you are following and that there will be no job offer made during the first or second interview. You should, in fact, share that bit of information with the candidate so she knows what to expect.

The First Interview (Ten to Twenty Minutes)

Getting to know the candidate during a brief tour of your store should be the focus of the first interview. This allows you to gain a feeling about how the candidate responds to your business. Introduce the candidate to other employees. How does this candidate respond to them? Is she friendly or standoffish? Watching how this person acts toward your current employees may give you an indication of how she would work as a part of your staff. As you tour the store, you can also give the candidate a general job description and let her ask questions of you.

After the brief tour (about five to ten minutes) ask her if she would like to fill out an application, if she hasn't already. If the candidate asks if she can take the application home, kindly but firmly tell her that you require all employment applications be filled out at the facility. If she insists, be firm. Clearly instruct her to fill out the entire application, sign it and bring it to you when she is finished. You can tell a lot about how sharp an applicant is by how long she takes to fill out an application and how accurate she is in completing it. See if she follows your instructions clearly. This is your first opportunity to test her. If she takes too long to fill out the application, or it is not properly or clearly filled out, then you know something more about the candidate.

Briefly review the application for completeness and then invite the candidate back for the second interview if you still feel she is a good prospect to join your team. The second interview is an important time to find out the details and should be done before or after business hours. Give the applicant a choice of days, but set the time for thirty minutes before opening or after closing. This way you won't be interrupted, and you can focus on the interview.

Before you begin the second interview, you'll need to follow a very important rule. I call it the 70/30 rule, which means that the candidate should talk seventy percent of the time during the interview while you only talk thirty percent of the time. This becomes more difficult to adhere to when you really like the candidate and want to hire her on the spot. But be aware—if you talk most of the time during the interview and invest all your time convincing the candidate that yours is the best place to work, how will you gather the information you need to make the most informed decision about the person being right for your company?

The Second Interview (Thirty Minutes)

The second interview is when you determine if the candidate has the skills and attitudes needed to become a productive employee in your business. Properly done, it should only take about thirty minutes

We always recommend to our clients that they prepare a list of standardized questions that will assist them in the interview process and keep them from asking questions that may not be appropriate. Questions should always focus on the candidate's ability to do the job and help you uncover their aptitudes, drives and motivations. Do not ask questions that allow the candidate to answer with a simple "yes" or "no." Don't just accept what a candidate says on the surface. Learn to dig into the answers and find out what they really mean.

Many questions are inappropriate and are, in fact, illegal to ask during the interviewing process. These are questions regarding marital status, race or religious beliefs. If you are not sure what questions you should be asking, contact your state Equal Employment Opportunity office for guidance.

The Third and Final Interview (Thirty Minutes)

The final interview happens only after you have gone through the first two interviews, checked references and found the candidate you are looking for. It is a time to make the candidate the official offer of employment and give her any paperwork to fill out as well as an orientation package, if you have one. Be sure to comply with all the normal employment forms and registrations. Remember that the job of hiring isn't done until the paperwork is finished.

These recruiting and interviewing steps may seem time-consuming and tedious on the surface; after all, it's quicker to just talk to someone for a few minutes, use your instincts and offer him or her a job. The problem is you can't make the best hiring decisions based on limited information. By following the processes for profiling, recruiting and interviewing, you will be investing your time wisely and will have an opportunity to hire the people who will bring life to your customer service systems.

New Employee Orientation

Once a new employee has been hired, the most import work can begin—bringing the employee into your business vision and training him to be a valuable asset to you, your customers and the other employees.

One of the inevitable facts of running any retail business is that you will have a certain amount of employee turnover. For some people, the idea of having to hire and train another new

Customer Service Is A Contact Sport™

employee is enough to make them want to stay home for the day. For others, it's just an unfortunate part of the job. And for others still, it is an opportunity to work with someone new and have fun doing it. Hiring and training new employees will always be part of any retail business, and the sooner one gets comfortable with the process, the sooner it will become fun—or at least not a situation to avoid.

Let me tell you a story that will illustrate the importance of new employee orientation. Several years ago, a friend of mine shared an experience that his teenage daughter had gone through. As a seventeen-year-old, one of her first summer jobs was working in a locally owned fast food restaurant. She hated the work. She felt that she was not good at it, did not enjoy the people she worked with, and she felt that the owner always seemed to be on her case for not doing the job right. She decided she did not like the job and quit within two weeks. A couple of days later, her friend told her she should apply at the restaurant where she (the friend) was working. My friend's daughter immediately declined, saying that she would never work in a fast food restaurant again. Her friend persisted, saying how much fun she had at work and how nice her boss was. Finally, the friend convinced her to put in an application.

My friend's daughter ended up taking the job. After a few days, her father asked her how she liked it, and she responded that she loved it! Surprised by her answer, her father inquired about what was different at this fast food restaurant. She told how organized the first few days on the job had been, how easy the training was and how everyone made her feel comfortable and liked. She was having fun at a business she said she would never be part of again. The new employee orientation and training that was provided made the difference in this employee, as it will with most.

Bringing a new employee onto your staff should be as easy as drawing a picture by connecting the dots. Maybe you remember doing some of these drawings when you were a child, or maybe you do them now with your own children. The concept is quite easy, and it's not that different when it comes to orienting and training a new employee.

First, we'll assume you have hired the right person and that he has the basic skills and aptitudes for the job. A properly structured new employee orientation will not make up for someone lacking the proper skill sets, so make sure you have hired and are orienting the best candidate you can find.

The next thing you should do before sitting down with a new employee is have a checklist. This document is nothing more than a list of what you normally do to familiarize a new employee with your business and make the first few days on the job more comfortable and productive. If you don't already have one, you will need to create one. Whatever it is that you do in your business on that first day, jot it down. Having these items in checklist form makes them more organized and clear. That way you won't forget anything important, and it will actually be easier to review the information with the new employee.

If you find that you are not sure what you do that makes a new employee comfortable, ask your most recent hire what you did with him. You may find some interesting answers. Maybe you didn't do so well. If that's the case, ask what you could have done to make the experience better.

It has probably been a long time since many of us have started a new job. It's easy to forget that there can often be a little (and sometimes a lot) of stress associated with a new job, new people, new processes and new experiences; so be sensitive, be prepared and have some fun.

What Vision Will You Share With Your New Employee?

An effective orientation should include sharing with the new employee the philosophies you have established for the business, especially those related to customer service. If you haven't communicated those ideas to your existing employees, now is the time to go back and do it.

All of your employees must know where you ultimately want the business to go, how you expect to get there and the role they will play. Do not assume they know. Here is an easy test to find out what your employees know about the vision, goals and customer service philosophies of the business. Ask them, "What is the customer service vision for this business, and what part do you play in helping to achieve it?" The answers, or lack thereof, may surprise you.

Be sure to let your new employee know your specific thoughts on how you will achieve the high level of customer service you have illustrated for him. Having a clear vision for how you want your employees to interact with the business and your customers is a vital first step in establishing your expectations and inspiring everyone to make it happen. It should be shared with the new employee in the first days of his employment.

If you made the right hire, your new employee is most likely ready to learn and eager to please you with a job well done. Unfortunately, this is where many business owners fall short. They do not take the time to properly train a new employee and establish the standards that will help him or her to succeed in the new job. Without the proper foundation, standards and expectations, it becomes more difficult for new hires to be comfortable with their responsibilities, and therefore, they will not be as successful.

Training Is More Than Telling

Many owners and managers take just enough time with employees to tell them what to do, never taking the time to train them and assure they are actually learning.

The ongoing challenge of developing skills and training employees to perform a job consistently and with excellence is something that every operator of every business faces at some point and to some degree. This is not an issue confined to retail, nor is it something you can fix all at once. However, if you observe the most successful retail companies, you will find that virtually all of them have one priority in common—a commitment to training and retraining their employees

Training should not just consist of you simply telling the employee to follow you around and ask questions. To be sure, learning by watching is fine for some tasks, but it should not take the place of a structured learning process.

We All Learn Differently

Employees are people, and people learn differently than each other. For those of you with children, you know that even siblings growing up in the same household have different personalities and learn their lessons differently. One child may be asked only once to clean up her room before she does it. Yet, you may have to ask her sibling several times, and his room still never gets cleaned.

In both cases, you have told them to clean their rooms, but maybe you needed to go further with the one child and spend some time counseling and training him. The reasons he doesn't clean the room, or doesn't clean it properly, can be as varied as the differences between people. Similarly, the job trainer needs to employ varied methods to produce the desired results. Since businesses and people change constantly, your methods of training and employee development should be reviewed continuously and adjusted to fit the particular employee or situation.

Kids, Pets and Your Employees

Speaking of kids, when my wife and I were blessed with the birth of our son, Taylor, we knew relatively nothing about raising or caring for an infant. However, as new parents of our first child, we committed to reading a fair amount about children and parenting. Being a professional trainer and communicator, I was especially interested in the information related to learning and skills development.

As I read more and experienced first-hand the daily learning situations in raising a child, I was surprised to find how similarly adults and children learn. Often we assume that because someone reaches adulthood, all we have to do is tell him what to do, and he will comply. Wouldn't that be nice? However, it is a well-documented fact that most people learn how to learn and develop their personalities and base communication styles before they reach their fifth birthday, long before they come to work for you. Some people learn to cooperate for the common good of the group, while others buck the system and rebel against even the mildest assertion of authority—just like kids!

Reading about these learning situations reminded me of an experience a few years before my son's birth—when we bought a puppy and hired a professional trainer to help us develop the proper habits and demeanor of that new addition to our family. I remember the first appointment with our trainer, who was known as a top dog trainer in our area. He was a quiet man, yet you could immediately sense his firm but gentle communication style. Within just a few moments, he had the jumping puppy completely under his control and lying next to him quietly.

However, when my wife, Terri, tried the "down" and "sit" commands, our little puppy looked at her with his big brown eyes, ignored her commands and started jumping and licking her hands and face. She tried her best to negotiate the puppy into the proper behavior, which is when our trainer made the statement I will always remember. He said to Terri, "The problem isn't your dog not wanting to listen. The problem is you are not willing to take the posture of being in control." He explained that our dog could sense her willingness to negotiate with him and was perfectly happy to allow her to let him have his way. He went on to explain that although dogs and people are different in most every way, there are some similarities in how we all learn, specifically with issues like clarity, consistency and resolve.

Allow me to expand on these three key components of training:

Clarity

Often what we say isn't what people hear. Have you ever participated in the communication exercise in which a sentence is whispered from one person to the next to illustrate basic communications dynamics? It's amazing that by the time the statement, "peanut butter and jelly sandwich" goes from one person to the next, the people at the end of the line are saying, "steak sandwich with mayo." Didn't everyone hear precisely what was said? Who changed the sentence?

If you look more closely at the dynamic, it isn't so much that people didn't hear what was said but that they paraphrased what they heard before they passed the statement on to their neighbor. This is similar to when you say to an employee, "We need to greet every customer immediately when they come into the store." But by the time this statement gets passed around a few times, the message has become, "Get to them as soon as you can." The moral of this lesson: be very clear about what you want.

Consistency

Touted by nearly every parent and training professional as one of the most important aspects of development and training, consistency plays a significant role in establishing acceptable behaviors and expectations. If an expectation is established and behaviors are set, and the trainee strays from the standard and you do nothing to bring it to her attention, then you're saying that other levels of behavior are acceptable. If you establish a guideline, process, rule or other standard, you must be consistent in expecting those behaviors and standards. What is acceptable today should be the standard for future behavior. If it is not acceptable today, then it should not be acceptable tomorrow. To not be consistent makes it impossible for the trainee to consistently meet your expectations and therefore will create confusion and problems with what is acceptable.

Resolve

This component is the commitment you make to any standard or process you feel is important to the overall success of your objectives. However, for resolve to be effective, it must be communicated to those who it will affect. For example, you may tell a child that she is not allowed to touch a particular item in your home and that if she does, there will be a consequence. When and if she does what she is not supposed to do, the consequence must be applied. If it is not, then you have said, in essence, "It is okay to do whatever you would like, and the consequence will not be forthcoming."

In another example, if you say that customer service is highly important to the success of your business and that every customer will be greeted with a smile, and if an employee doesn't comply, and you don't correct the behavior, you have basically said, "It is okay to not greet every customer with a smile." Resolve is like a promise to yourself and others that whatever the commitment you have made, it will be kept at all cost.

Motivation

Most people want to believe that if someone knows how to do something, he or she will then do it. But this isn't always the case. Look at this same issue from a training perspective; just because you take the time to train an employee for a task doesn't mean that he will do it.

I hear all too often from business owners and managers who share with me their frustrations about not being able to motivate their employees. They say they tell their employees what to do but that the employees just don't seem to get it or don't seem to care. The reality is most people do get it, and they do care. The real issue is that people do what's important to them. And therein is one of the greatest mysteries and challenges of motivating your employees. How do you make what is important to you and the business important to them?

Motivation is not an easy thing for some business owners. I hear supervisors complaining that their people are not motivated to do their best, or they feel they always need to be on their employees' backs to get the job done. Unfortunately, there is no pill that will create sustainable motivation in an employee. It must come from within the individual.

Maybe you have had an employee whom you couldn't motivate to properly present a product, but when it came to a conversation about anything he was personally motivated about, he became highly motivated. This illustration proves my point that people do what is important to them. Rarely do you find a person who is not motivated about something.

The key to helping motivate someone is to make the result of an act important to her. Simply telling her, "It's your job" does not necessarily make it important, nor does it serve as a motivator. Take time to find out what is valuable or pertinent to individual employees and use that to generate and reinforce the desired behavior.

W I F M (What's In It For Me?)

"What's in it for me?" is a basic question we all ask at some point. I don't like it, but it's how many people motivate. For some, it is necessary to show how doing something is going to help them in the future; others need to see how something will have an immediate impact. In all cases, you need to balance meeting present needs and building future values. Think of a starving person searching for food. Telling him how to plant, nurture and harvest does not meet his immediate needs. But only feeding him today does not help him prepare for the future. The best approach is to address your employees' immediate needs and also help them prepare for the future.

Would You Like To Work For You?

Despite what many people think, money is not the primary motivator of most people. Yes, money—especially bonus programs—can help your employees focus on activities like selling products or making quotas, but such programs cannot substitute for a drive to do the right thing and a focus on excellence. People need money to take care of basic financial needs and to support their chosen lifestyle, but true motivation cannot be bought with money alone.

Think about the factors that motivate people:
- appreciation
- recognition
- being a part of a special team
- a sense of accomplishment
- commitment
- (and yes) material rewards

Sometimes, looking at what causes people to become unmotivated helps to clarify what would motivate them:
- being yelled at
- being ridiculed
- lack of appreciation
- being taken for granted
- not having the opportunity to experience the feeling of success

The process of motivating your employees becomes easier if the work environment is conducive to positive thinking and enthusiasm. Motivating people is about creating an environment and a relationship between you, your people and the business that is mutually beneficial to all the parties involved.

Be aware of what your employees are doing. Pay attention to their needs, acknowledge when they do things right, and compliment them on their accomplishments. If you lay out the expectations you have for their performance and the structure to help them achieve it, you will find your people being more motivated.

To help you understand if you are addressing some of the base motivational components for your employees, review the following checklist:

Motivation Basics
- Communicate the vision for your company
- Encourage peak performance
- Motivate by example
- Reward good performance
- Be sincere/be around
- Be respectful toward your staff
- Make your business fun
- Talk about the future

This is not a complete checklist of every motivational factor in your business, and these may not work in every situation, especially if you are trying to motivate someone who just doesn't have a desire to succeed. However, these suggestions will help you to create a more motivationally focused environment, and they will help your employees to become positive assets to your business and to be more satisfied with their jobs.

Training Is A Process, Not An Event!

One of the most important skills an owner or manager of a business can develop is the ability to train his staff and help them achieve the highest level of their potential. Whether you are training employees to greet customers, to properly demonstrate a product or to perform a detailed technical process, there are some specific procedures that will help you train better and enable your employees to learn more completely.

Training employees requires time and commitment. However, most training is usually thought of as an event that occurs and then ends. In reality, learning should be a process that happens over time. Approaching training as a process instead of an event gives a business owner more realistic expectations of the training as well as an opportunity to support and reinforce the knowledge and skills he wants his employees to learn. Ultimately, it makes training more effective.

The entire concept of training is nothing more than communicating to others the standards and processes that will lead to a specific result and then helping them do the activities that will accomplish the objectives.

How Important Is Training To You?

Is it important enough for you to assign a budget for employee training and education? Most everyone says training is important, but an interesting fact is that few business owners spend any time (much less money) on what is probably the *most* important part of their business component.

Let's compare the importance of training to the importance of advertising. Advertising is a key component of a successful marketing program and can help get customers to come to your center. Most businesses even have an advertising budget or at least an idea of how much they can spend on advertising. But doesn't it make more sense to be sure the operation and facility you are inviting the customer to is the best it can be? Advertising will help you get a customer into your store the first time, but it is outstanding customer service, supported by effective training, that will assure they return again and again.

Not investing in training would be like spending money on advertising a restaurant that doesn't have good food or service. Wouldn't it make sense to first get the kitchen, wait staff and dining area up to speed? Then the customers that do come in (because of the advertising) would have an experience that would assure repeat business.

How much emphasis do you put on training in your company? Our most successful clients have it at the top of their list, and it is a budgeted item. Depending on the size of your business and your length of time in business, you should budget from two to three percent of annual sales. That means if you are generating $500,000 in sales per year you should be investing a minimum of $15,000 in training-related programs. This might include industry-related training materials, books, manuals, tapes or seminars. It should also include your annual trip to an industry convention. Whatever training programs you decide to invest your training dollars in, I can assure you this—the return on investment will be much greater and more long term than any advertisement you have ever run.

By the way, I recommend putting your training investment into a separate account so you avoid spending it on non-training-related items. If it is kept in your general account, you could easily spend it on other capital items. Don't shortchange your investment in training.

About The Coach—You!

There is little difference between coaching a business team and coaching a championship sports team. Coaching any team that is motivated to win is a lot more fun than trying to motivate players who don't care whether they win or lose.

As important as the player is to the success of the team, the player's primary responsibility is to carry out the specifics of his position. It is the job of the coach, however, to develop the game plan and the skills in the players and on game day make sure the plan is followed precisely. Along the way comes a commitment to "practice, practice and more practice" to refine the skills that will lead to winning results. And to be sure, anything less than 100 percent effort can only produce less than 100 percent results.

Even the best players need to be inspired by the coach from time to time so they can keep the winning effort moving forward. No player can be at the highest level day in and day out. Almost every sport has examples of coaches who inherit mediocre teams, then set out with an improved game plan and inspired players and win championships. The coach is important, indeed.

Don't Forget About Training You!

Once in business, the need for information and education becomes critically important; however, the time allowed for learning is limited due to the pressures and constraints of running a business. Just understanding the issues related to employee performance and motivation can be a daunting task, but add to that the ongoing marketing challenges, daily operations problems and a changing list of priorities and you can quickly see how the need for information and structure is so pronounced. Let us not forget that learning is literally a matter of life and death for your business.

Most business owners have families and a number of other obligations that demand their time and attention. It may seem as though you do not have the time to learn more skills that will help you to manage a successful business, but the truth is you need to invest the time. You only have twenty-four hours per day to achieve your best return for your business, so the issue isn't really making more time but optimizing the time you do have.

Although the big yellow bus has stopped coming, we must not stop seeking learning situations. Are you actively seeking new ideas every day to improve some aspect of your business? Are you testing and practicing new processes that will help streamline operations or improve customer service or maybe increase your marketing efforts? As a professional consultant, I have the opportunity to help people improve their businesses, and I often hear clients admit they are stuck in a rut. They tell me that they have stopped learning about their businesses and actively seeking new ways to do business. Sure, if someone hit them over the head with a new idea they may respond, but that is a far cry from actively seeking new ideas, processes and methods.

Learning how to be more successful in your business is not that difficult and doesn't have to take any additional time, if done on a daily basis. It can be as simple as making a commitment to being more observant while you are out being a customer or reading a business book instead of a novel.

There Is No Saturation Point In Education

Our brains are not capable of reaching the point where they can't accept more information. We can always learn more. We all are constantly being exposed to new information. What we do with the information is a matter of choice, and how we use it determines the results we get.

Ideas Give You Options

The more concepts and ideas you expose yourself to, the more information you have at your disposal to make informed decisions. You don't always have to buy every aspect of a new concept or idea you hear about; maybe just part of the concept works for you. For example, we have a detailed technician and manager compensation model we suggest that our clients use. Many use the program exactly as we submit it, although I have seen some very good variations on the model.

A note of caution: I have often seen someone take a basic and effective program and complicate it so much that it does not produce the results for which it was designed. The issue here is that there are usually ways to improve on what you do. We all need other people's ideas and input.

Learning Happens Everyday

Learn from everyone. Watch how others serve you at a restaurant, a car dealership or a clothing store. Observe people speaking to their customers. How do the employees greet them? How do they take care of special requests or handle complaints? You will see some things done right and some things wrong. It is interesting that seeing someone miss an opportunity to help a customer can be just as much of a learning experience as watching someone do it the right way. Be open to new ideas and concepts that can help you improve your business. You never know when the next great business idea will cross your path.

Focus Training On What You Are Trying To Improve

This sounds so fundamental, but I often see companies that talk about an area needing improvement yet have no training in place to make the improvements happen. Take the airline industry. The majority of the companies talk about customer service being a core value, yet according to numerous interviews we have conducted with flight attendants, less than five percent of the training a flight attendant receives focuses on customer service. No wonder most airlines are well known for their low levels of customer service.

Develop The Culture

This includes hiring the right people. If you hire people who see the vision for your company and instill in them how important excellence is in every aspect of your business, you achieve the vision much faster than you thought possible. Developing the culture of your business is important to creating the daily dynamics and synergies that can help any business achieve the highest levels of performance. One thing is for sure—the wrong people never make the right culture happen.

Be An Excellent Example

Supporting the culture in your organization requires that you live as an excellent example of how you want your business and your employees to be perceived by your customers on a daily basis. The business world is full of companies that have risen to the highest levels of success, not because of some great new widget but because the people in that organization have done everything with excellence and a spirit of enthusiasm. The culture of the business and the spirit of the team are at the very foundation of every successful business.

The steps outlined in this chapter are critically important, but they are only part of a comprehensive employee recruiting and training program that should be developed and implemented in your business. Never stop learning.

Chapter Four Summary
- Profiling - hire attitude, train competence
- Recruiting - be active about looking
- Interviewing - follow the process
- Training - training is more than telling
- Motivation - people do what's important to them
- Develop the culture
- Be an excellent example

Customer Service Is A Contact Sport™

Chapter Five

Facility Imaging And Merchandising

Image isn't everything, but it is very important to many of your customers.

The second of the three critical components you must focus on to attain the highest level of customer service excellence is your facility—the place your customers go when they visit your business. Whether it is a shoe store, restaurant or automotive facility, you have an opportunity to create a positive impact on your customers. From the showroom and displays, counters, floors and restrooms to signage, lighting, room temperature and background music, everything your customer comes in contact with contains the seeds of a positive or negative experience.

Everything You Do Creates An Impact

Many customers place a high value on a clean, orderly business but also one that is customer-focused. A cup of coffee, current and interesting magazines and a clean, comfortable place to wait all work toward creating a positive impact on your customer. These little things go a long way toward establishing great customer relations. I have a saying that I use in trying to communicate this point to a client: retail is detail. Those businesses that take care of the details win more customers than those that don't.

An interesting point to remember about the retail business is that your customer is a person. This sounds basic enough, but that is precisely what makes retailing, and especially customer service, so complex and dynamic. It also provides you with great challenges and opportunities. Everything you do makes an impact; you have no choice about the matter. Your only choice is whether the impact you create will be a positive or negative one. You can choose to have a well-organized store or to keep it dirty and unattractive. Each approach will have its own impact. Which one do you want created in your customer's mind?

In this chapter, I will discuss three basic aspects of your business model that create impressions with your customers: the exterior of your business, the interior of your store and your employees.

The Exterior

If your business is located in a mall, a strip shopping center or a larger national chain store, most of the exterior considerations are taken care of by someone else. However, if you are an independent business owner or in a stand-alone building, you may have to create the image of the facility on your own. (Even in such a case, much of how your signage looks will be governed by your local municipality or some other entity.) While I could write an entire book on the subject of exterior imaging alone, here are some of the main factors to consider when creating the visual elements of your business's exterior.

Exterior signage is critical to letting your customers know your business is available to them. Equally important is the message it conveys to your customer beyond the words. For

Facility Imaging And Merchandising

example, is the signage well kept and clean? Is it well lighted? Does it effectively add to the image of your business in such a way that it invites and inspires a customer to come inside?

Landscaping is another imaging point. If you have landscaping, is it well maintained? Have you taken advantage of opportunities to use color in the landscape design? Are there flowers, mulch and shrubs? If you have a lawn, is it green and healthy, or is it dead? Are there more weeds than grass? Is there litter strewn about? A well-manicured facility speaks volumes to a customer about what she might expect inside the business.

I remember reading a story about Ray Kroc, the founder of the McDonald's restaurant chain. Legend has it that even in his later years of life, Mr. Kroc would have his driver stop his car near any McDonald's he would visit, and if there was litter on the property, Mr. Kroc would personally pick up every piece of paper he saw. He felt strongly about keeping the grounds around that restaurant free of litter or anything else that would distract from the visual appeal of the business. He would take the bag full of papers and trash, march right into the manager's office and set it on his desk. Not much else needed to be said, but I am sure his point was made. I admire Ray Kroc for his commitment to what he believed and his dramatic way of making his point.

Lighting at night is also important for many businesses. If your company has outdoor visibility, guess what? On most days, it is dark for just as many hours as it is daylight. If your facility is not properly lit at night, then thousands of potential customers who normally only travel by your location at night are oblivious to the fact that your business even exists.

The Interior

The interior has much of the same potential to make an impact as the exterior does, In fact, because the customers are typically closer to everything while inside your store, the impression your interior makes is even more noticeable to them.

While decorating a business's interior is an individual choice and should reflect one's personal tastes, there are some imaging basics that must be adhered to. Beyond purely cosmetic elements like wallpaper and paint, a well-designed imaging package will address many other issues, including customer comfort and education. The proper imaging and merchandising touches will not only make for a more attractive environment but directly affect sales of additional products and services.

Wallpaper

Wallpaper is an inexpensive way to brighten up a customer waiting area or restroom. Choose a commercial grade, vinyl-backed wallpaper that is easy to clean and coordinates with the rest of the decor. Installing a chair rail near the seating area will help prevent chair backs from damaging the wallpaper over time.

Seating

If your business requires that customers be seated for any length of time, make sure they will be comfortable. The nature of your business will dictate to some degree the type of seating you can use; however, a few basics apply here as well. The upholstery on the seats should be a medium color that will not show dirt and normal wear and tear. A steel frame will last longer than wood and can withstand the rigors of commercial use. Arms on chairs in the customer waiting area are nice but not necessary.

Lighting

This area of interior design is almost completely overlooked. Consider using lights to highlight specific signs, which will help bring attention to the message being communicated. Lighting that is too bright or too dark can create a negative presentation. Observe the lighting in a dressing room at a clothing store; fluorescent lights are cheaper to install and maintain, but they make everyone look bad. Many upscale stores use softer, incandescent lights. If the idea is to have customers look and feel better about themselves and subsequently purchase the items they are trying on, consider the importance of proper lighting.

Plants

Plants can be an inexpensive way to add a touch of class and create a more inviting environment in a quick-lube facility, for example. To test the importance of this concept, try removing the plants from a room in your house for an afternoon and see how bare it becomes. We do suggest, however, that you avoid the maintenance that comes with real plants and use silk plants instead. A quality silk plant will look real and require no upkeep.

Coffee

Coffee is one of the most consumed beverages in our society. In fact, some coffee lovers are absolutely rabid about the quality of the products they consume. As with anything else you offer a customer, the coffee should be of the highest quality you can afford. To assure that it is properly brewed and kept hot, you should brew it in the store, in a commercial grade air pot. An air pot will keep the coffee from burning and help keep it hot and fresh for hours. Serve decaf for your non-caffeine customers.

Place a sign on each air pot identifying the brew and offer it to your customers with your compliments.

Restroom

For customers who care (and most do), the cleanliness of the restrooms is very important. The impression it conveys can make or break the other image components. Try to create an environment that is clean without being too sterile and warm without being too fluffy. Use wallpaper on at least one wall (commercial grade that is easily cleaned). Add a silk flower/plant arrangement for color. Make sure to stock all the paper products a customer would need along with plenty of soap and air freshener. Most importantly, keep the restroom as clean as possible, and don't use the restroom as a mop closet!

Signage and Displays

In today's competitive retail arena, it has become increasingly important to offer an ever-expanding range of services and products. This is driven not only by the business owner who needs to generate more revenue per transaction but by the consumer who wants and needs more products and services. With more choices for your customers comes the challenge of properly presenting the various offerings in a way that is clear and evident, without confusing the customer or appearing pushy. An effective merchandise presentation is not only more attractive but more comfortable and informative to your customer.

The objective of properly developed signage and displays should be to educate or motivate a customer to purchase a service or product and to understand more about your business

Facility Imaging And Merchandising

values. If you have ever had a customer ask for a service because she read about it in on a sign or brochure, then you have experienced the benefits of these merchandising tools.

Signs are one of the standardized methods of communicating information to your customers; in fact, they are often called the "silent sales person." Done effectively, they can account for as much as five to fifteen percent of sales and can support the sales efforts of virtually every service or product you offer. If you have a message you want to consistently convey, decide on the most effective way to communicate that message, capture it with a sign and let that sign do its job for all your future customers.

Because there are so many different types of retail businesses, I couldn't possibly cover all the details of the specific messages you could and should have. In-store signage, however, typically includes posters, brochures and banners. Be sure that any interior signage is professionally printed and attractive and not handwritten. Don't fall into the trap of trying to communicate too many messages on one sign; likewise, if too many signs are posted, none of them will get the attention it should have. Less is more.

Product displays can also be powerful and attention-getting. An attractive display will draw customers to read the message. Literature and promotional support at these displays will drive home your message and educate your customers. Professionally produced videos can be a powerful tool as well. Many of our clients use custom-designed videotapes to educate customers. This medium is interactive and, therefore, more powerful. Customers who are waiting for services are a captive audience for a video that talks about a company's newest or most popular products or services. A video may not necessarily sell the customer on the spot, but it could very well plant the seed for buying a product or service on the next visit.

Employees

Your work force is the most dynamic and difficult aspect of your business to maintain. Here's a story that illustrates the importance of employee image:

Recently, I needed an oil change for my car, so I stopped at an oil change facility close to our corporate offices. Even though the location was the closest to my office and home, I had never had my oil changed there; I had always gone to another store that was farther away because I knew the owner.

Within a few seconds of driving up to the service bay doors, a young man approached my car. I noticed that instead of a uniform he was wearing a faded, blue T-shirt with a huge hole ripped in the belly, his paunchy, hairy belly protruding through. The shirt was not tucked into his pants, and, as is the style with many young people, his jeans were at least three to four waist sizes too big and the crotch hung down around his knees. I would expect this of a kid hanging at the mall, but it wasn't the kind of image that projected experience and professionalism at an auto service business.

After telling him I wanted an oil change, he instructed me to leave the car, that he would get to it in about fifteen minutes. At that point I had to make a decision about whether or not I wanted to turn my car over to this kid. Nothing about his appearance or his presentation of the service made me confident in his abilities. He did not look like a professional, and nothing he said made me feel that he cared or was trained properly. I had no reason to trust him with servicing my car. I made a decision that thousands of potential customers make every day and left

Facility Imaging And Merchandising

without buying that service. This is known as the "fight or flight" syndrome. I didn't feel like dealing with a potential problem (fight), so I chose the easier of the two options and took flight.

Later, I thought more about why I had left without getting my car serviced. I realized the judgment I made wasn't based on that young man's ability to do an oil change (I didn't even know what his level of experience and competence was) but on how that person or the owner of the facility might have handled a problem with my car. If the owner did not care enough to provide proper uniforms and training to his employee, then I surely would not want to be on the opposing end of a service problem with him.

I am sure you have heard the old adage "perception is reality." I don't think that's true. Perception and reality are often at opposite ends of the scale. My perception was that this technician was not experienced and that the owner did not care. The truth could very well have been that the technician was quite experienced and the owner cared a great deal. The problem was that I never got to know the truth and could only rely on my first impressions and instincts to guide me. Yes, I could have watched over them like a hawk to make sure they did the service properly, but was that really what I wanted to do?

How could this situation have gone differently? To start, the technician could have been in a proper uniform. A ripped T-shirt and sloppy jeans do not inspire feelings of confidence. Second, the tech should have been trained in a proper greeting and service presentation. Anyone greeting customers must know how to present the service in its best light and do so in a manner that is friendly and engaging. In this scenario, perception became my reality, and I never went back to get my car serviced there. Does this sound harsh and judgmental? It if does, all I can say is, "Welcome to retail." The TV ad slogan that said, "You only get one chance to make a good first impression" definitely applied to this situation.

At a recent social gathering, I overheard a friend of mine sharing an experience about a plumber who had provided exceptional service. Not only had he been on time to the appointment and fixed the problem, but he had been polite and customer-focused. She was most impressed with the professionalism with which the plumber conducted himself. She commented on his clean and pressed uniform and the fact that he even wore cotton booties after he took his shoes off so he wouldn't get her carpets dirty. He even wore latex gloves. These extra precautions not only served as operational solutions to assure the customer's home was protected but were impressive from a customer care perspective. The plumber's extra preparation paid off. My friend raved about the service and said she would definitely recommend this plumber to others.

More On Uniforms

Everywhere you turn you see uniforms—from plumbers and waiters to automotive service technicians and computer repair techs. In most cases, they are a well-thought-out part of a businesses image. In other cases, they are just an afterthought—something to keep the employee's personal clothes from getting dirty.

Recently, the bank that my wife and I use asked all of its tellers to wear red sweater vests featuring the bank's logo (the officers and account representatives were not outfitted in them since they were required to wear suits). As I stood in line, I noticed how sharp all the tellers looked. Some were only in their early twenties, and a couple were quite a bit older, yet they all had an orderly and neat appearance. It standardized the imaging behind the counter, it made the tellers look more professional, and it made the rest of the interior decor more attractive. The right uniform, worn well and maintained properly, will have a positive effect on customers. Many customers may not consciously notice, but on a more subliminal level, the right uniform will convey professionalism and organization.

Another bank I know of in our area does not require its tellers to wear uniforms. The outfits in which I sometimes see the tellers dressed— low rise pants, midriff tops, jeans—do not speak of standardization. In fact, they display a lack of standards, which goes hand-in-hand with sloppiness. These are not people you want to trust with your money and investments.

Uniforms can have many different looks—from a pressed and starched shirt and pants to a more relaxed golf shirt and cotton trousers. Every business has to decide for itself what works for its specific environment. One thing is for sure—uniforms should be *uniform* (the word itself means sameness or similarity) not a mismatch of colors and styles.

If your business lends itself to your employees wearing uniforms, what do they look like? Do they support a professional image? Do they coordinate with your facility's color scheme? Are they clean? Well-kept? These are all important questions if you are to put your best image forward every day, with every customer.

Your Customer's Sensory Perceptions

Let's focus for a moment on each of the sensory impacts your business has on your customers: sight, sound, smell, touch and taste.

Sight

This applies to every retail business. Customers see many things and develop perceptions from those visuals. For instance, is your store organized? Does everything have a place? Does it appear orderly and clean? Is the inventory easy to locate? Is it neat and fresh? Are there desks, countertops, storage bins or shelves that need to be cleared and cleaned?

What about work spaces? There are many books written on how to keep desks and work areas organized and efficient. Maybe you have even read some of them. Some consider desks personal space and will not even consider the suggestion they organize theirs. While that may carry some weight in an office environment, it is not acceptable anywhere in a retail facility, especially where customers can see these areas and draw conclusions about the quality of your business.

Don't forget that your work staff is part of this visual component. Do your employees appear to know what they are doing, or do they seem unsure of how to process some part of the customer transaction? Are they enthusiastic and energetic or dreary and bored? Do they stand around and wait for the customer to approach them, or do they engage the customer? All these visuals make an impression and have an impact.

Sound

What sounds do your customers hear while visiting your business? Employee conversations, pleasant background tones and tense conversations on the telephone are all influences that can and should be controlled.

Music can have either a positive or negative impact on your customer's visit, depending on the music selection and the customer demographic. It should be selected to create an atmosphere that is conducive to customer service. I suggest staying in the middle of the road when it comes to music style; most people do not object to an easy listening station. In any case, music should not be selected based solely on you employees' tastes and personal preferences.

The lack of music can have a more negative impact. Try turning off all the sound in your store and listening to the deafening quiet. When a customer comes into that kind of an environment, it can be intimidating and uncomfortable for him or her. The right music, at the right volume, can lend an air of movement and energy that will match up just right with your imaging and business presentation.

Some stores have televisions in their display areas. What I typically observe on televisions in retail businesses ranges from news shows to "shock" talk shows to soap operas. (Some of the soap operas I have seen on these publicly viewed televisions are so racy they almost demand an "R" rating. They feature violence, deception and people hopping in bed with other people's spouses.) Consider the many customers who come to your business with young children. Are sensationalized sex and violence the values you want to convey to your customers and their children? Instead, consider the many other positive functions of a TV in a retail store—educational television, customized communications designed to educate your customers or even peaceful visual scenes.

Smell

Smells can be some of the most attractive or repulsive sensory stimuli your customers come in contact with at your business. What do your patrons smell when they step through the front doors—the sweet smell of flowers, the repulsive odor of chemicals or the foul smell of stale smoke? Customers easily can turn their eyes in another direction, try not to listen to a noise or avoid touching or tasting something, but they must breathe and, subsequently, smell.

There are many ways to create pleasant smells in your customer environment. Spraying lightly scented fragrances is both appealing and inexpensive. Just be sure to refresh the spray as needed. More natural delivery methods include flowers, freshly ground coffee and—a method we used in residential home sales—a couple of drops of vanilla extract in a warm oven. It conjures up the smell of someone baking. Be aware that whatever delivery method you choose, be sure the fragrance is not overpowering, as this can be just as offensive as a foul odor. With fragrance, a bit less is better than too much.

Do whatever is necessary to avoid foul odors in a place of business. I remember a hobby shop where the owners smoked so heavily behind the counter, you almost couldn't breathe. Without getting into health issues and other potential hazards of smoking, it's fair to say that customers who are even mildly offended by smoke would avoid this hobby shop like the plague. I couldn't imagine a parent bringing his child in to shop at such a place. There are too many other hobby shops he could visit without subjecting himself to this negative impact. As it turns out, that is just what the customers of this particular shop did; they went elsewhere for their hobby needs. Needless to say, that hobby shop is now out of business.

Touch

Nothing repulses people more than touching something sticky, dirty or slimy. If a customer sits in a chair and gets dirty, I assure you that she will never go back to that store again. The

Facility Imaging And Merchandising

same outcome could occur when a customer leans against a dirty counter or table. Customers also measure a store by how clean its restrooms are. Interestingly, if a restroom is moderately clean, not too many people will notice. However, if it is abnormally dirty or spotlessly clean, people will take mental notes, and it becomes part of the overall impression they associate with your business.

In a restaurant, being clean is critical since people associate the cleanliness of the tables, utensils, seats, floors, etc., with the sanitation and safety of the food. If a grocery market offers apples with dust on them, it doesn't matter that the fruit inside is fresh and sweet; if the outside looks bad, no one will buy them. Dust, dirt and grime even create negative impressions when it comes to things people will not personally consume. Think about the retail shoe store trying to sell the "hot" item on the shelf, and the shoes on display are covered in dust.

Taste

This is the killer for restaurants. If people don't like the food, the game is over. But many other businesses offer consumables (such as coffee) to their customers as well. My opinion has always been that if you are going to offer something to your customer, offer the best. Don't serve burnt "mud" coffee. Serve the freshest brew you possibly can. Pour it into a carafe or air pot, and don't let it burn on the warmer plate. The coffee will stay fresher longer, and it will make the positive impression you are looking for. Whether it is coffee, tea, biscotti, candy or popcorn, if it is worth offering to your customer it is worth doing it right.

Remember, making your customer comfortable will also help boost add-on revenues. Which amenities will make your customer most comfortable? It's hard to say because every customer is unique. However, the way you prepare the facility and the way your employees interact with customers will leave a significant impression. It is up to you to create a facility and service system that meets and exceeds your customers' expectations. There is no cut-and-dried, concrete solution to this challenge. It is a matter of personal preference, space limitations, cost and, most importantly, a desire to provide an environment in which your employees can best serve your customers with excellence.

In summary, ask yourself these questions: Is your store clean and well merchandised? Does the appearance and cleanliness of your facility suggest quality and organization? Is the customer restroom spotless? Is the facility comfortable for the customer, and are the proper amenities available? What are the colors, and what is the predominate theme, or look, of your business? How do your employees appear to the customers? Are they dressed in an appropriate style for the business you are in? From a merchandising standpoint, what displays or printed messages are the customers exposed to? Do they inform and educate your customer?

Remember, the best customers are the ones who are comfortable, sense all the little things that you do for them and know that you care and want to provide the very best in comfort, convenience and service.

Chapter Five Summary
- Everything you do creates an impact
- Employees are an animated part of your business impact
- Appeal to your customers' sensory perceptions

Chapter Six

The Systems Behind Great Customer Service

Systems control the service your customer will receive. Your employees give the systems personality and make them come alive.

The third component of excellent customer service is the systems and processes that serve as guidelines for your employees. This includes everything from your greeting to how you process a customer. It's not just the types of products and services you have available or how well you provide the physical service; equally as important is how the customer feels while he is receiving the service.

The customer service experience is controlled, and in many ways created, by the systems and processes you put in place. Think about a choreographed dance. To the audience there is no system, no process, just flow and beautiful movement. Every dancer is in her place at a specific time, making a specific movement. A total process happens at the right time to create the effect that has been carefully designed into the show. To the dancers, it is second nature—they have practiced and rehearsed for many hours to ensure that the audience receives an outstanding performance. Much like that dance, your best customer service needs to be part of a planned system that outlines what will happen, when it will happen and who will do it.

In your business, think about something as basic as the customer greeting. How are your customers greeted? When are they greeted and by whom? Does "friendly and engaging" describe the manner in which your customers are approached? What happens to make the customer feel welcomed in the business?

Although many of the items I mention in this chapter may sound more like attitude issues, they are part of the system and process that assures your customers are going to receive the most excellent service possible.

Operational Excellence

As nice and friendly as you may be to every customer who comes to your business, you are still expected to have the products or services that meet or exceed their needs. And rightly so; that is, after all, why they come to you in the first place. If you go to a clothing store to buy a suit, you expect the store to have a selection of suits in your size. If you drink decaf and go to a coffee shop, you expect to be able to get decaf. A customer who goes to a car wash expects to have a clean car when it comes out the end of the wash tunnel.

And since nearly all of us go to car washes on occasion, allow me to use a typical wash experience as an example of operational excellence. In the following scenario, notice all the opportunities at each step of the car wash process to deliver excellent customer service.

What does a customer see upon approaching a car wash? Is the facility clean, and is the perimeter area free of litter? Are the signs prominently displayed and easy to read? What is the message the business is communicating today? Is there signage that welcomes the customer and helps establish the service expectations? For example: "Welcome to XYZ Car Wash. Please take a moment to review our special packages. One of our friendly attendants will be with you in a moment to serve you." Another idea may be to offer a special service that a customer may not be thinking about at that moment. Example: "Road salt and sand are harmful to your vehicle's finish. Try our Silver Package that includes a special rinse and undercarriage wash." The signs should inform the customer of available options. By directing the customer to review the packages, sales will increase and she will know about added values being offered.

Next comes the greeting. How long does a customer wait before the attendant approaches? What does the customer see when she is approached by the attendant? Is he well groomed? What does he say? Is he smiling? Does he walk around the car first and then approach the customer's window and greet her with a friendly tone? Does he make suggestions on an upgraded wash based on the condition of the customer's car? When the attendant hands the customer a slip of paper to take to the cashier, does he tell the customer what to do, or does he assume that she has been there before and knows what to do and where to go?

Does the cashier just take the customer's money and give her change and a receipt? If a car wash is customer-focused, the owner/manager realizes there are many opportunities to market other services to the customer, such as detailing, waxing or even specials or clubs. This would be the ideal time for the cashier to be friendly and engaging.

It is always of interest to me when a customer watches her car go through the wash. How do the prep guys scrub the wheels and the dirtiest parts of the car? Do they look at the customer and acknowledge her? Do they take extra care to make sure everything is clean, and do they look like they are enjoying the work? Do the people who dry the car get the windows and not leave streaks on the exterior? Do they get the door jambs? Do they comment on the customer's car? Do they engage the customer? Is a quality inspection done on the car? Does someone hold the door open and tell the customer to have a nice day and invite her back?

When the customer leaves the facility, how does she feel about what she has just received? Of course, her car is clean, but how was she treated? Does she feel cared for, or was there a complete lack of customer care?

How many customers come through this wash and never have the opportunity to receive the best care for their cars? Customers trust that if their cars need something, you will tell them. It's another way to build trust into your customer relationship. Don't let the opportunity go by.

Watch For Signs

Remember that customers will send you signals about what they need. They come to your business with their own sets of schedules and commitments that have nothing to do with your business. For the customer who is in a hurry, make the effort to communicate to him the wait time or how you will do your best to expedite the service he has come to you for. If a customer walks in with a baby, open the door and offer to carry something for her. Go the extra mile to make sure she feels welcome. For the new customer, invest some extra time.

For example, if your business is an automotive service facility, explain the procedures that your technicians follow and any technical equipment used. If you run a clothing store, make sure you introduce yourself and let the customer know about any special sections you may have displayed. If you have any information that will help the customer see your business as interesting, unique or different, make sure he knows this information before he leaves. This may be the only chance you get to impress upon him the value of doing business with you.

Show Interest

One of the best ways to show a customer you are interested in her needs is to listen. This may sound like a basic fundamental that shouldn't even have to be mentioned, but you see it every day—customers talking and the employees not listening. To show a customer you are paying attention, you should always listen, acknowledge and respond.

When you are listening to what a customer is saying, are you *really* listening, or are you waiting for her to stop talking so you can talk? One thing you can do to let the customer know you are listening is "active listening." It means letting the customer know you are listening by nodding occasionally or otherwise acknowledging that you are paying attention to her. Responding is what you do after a customer has communicated with you.

As an example, let's say you go into a shoe store and, after looking at a display, a sales associate approaches. You ask to see a particular shoe in a size nine, and while you are speaking, the salesperson looks at you, nods, then says he will be right back after checking to see if he has a nine in stock. It's all easy and transparent to you, but it gives you the feedback you need. In the reverse of this interaction, the associate would not make eye contact and, after you made your request, would say nothing and walk away. You would have no idea if the associate even heard you correctly.

Customers like to be complimented, so do it. Find out something personal about them. Maybe one is wearing an attractive suit or has a great watch or is wearing a nice cologne or perfume. Be appropriate, of course, but reach out and say something nice to someone. If appropriate, ask what type of work the customer does. You may just stumble upon a common interest. Building rapport will go a long way in ensuring repeat business. Maybe the customer has a well-behaved child in tow. If so, ask permission (without the child hearing you) to give the child a balloon, soda, piece of candy, etc. Safety and cleanliness will be important to this customer as well, so provisions for a kid-friendly environment need to be addressed as well.

Recognizing Opportunities With Your Customers

When a customer comes into your business, do you see him or her as a person with a diverse set of individualized needs or just another transaction? I know most of us would like to think we do the former, but based on actual events that we have observed, most of us could improve our skills at recognizing opportunities that walk through our doors every day. For opportunity to be realized, it must first be recognized.

While bringing new customers to your business may be the ultimate goal of a marketing initiative, it may not be the place to start when you are trying to improve your overall business performance. Look at all the components of your business and make sure that the customers who are already coming to your business are being properly cared for. In doing so, you will assure that you retain a high level of loyal customers and that the people who are added to your customer base will not only come back for more but tell their friends about you.

Recently, I had the pleasure of listening to a speaker share his experiences visiting three different retail businesses. His general observation was that although everyone with whom he came in contact was pleasant and the services were delivered in a timely manner, no one ever made an effort to find out about him—what his specific needs were and if they could be met in an individualized way. The better job you do at identifying and filling specific customer needs, the more appreciative your customers are. Although we will cover more about customer surveys in a later chapter, here are some customer motivations to identify:

- Is this his/her first time into your business?
- Why did he/she choose you?
- Where does this person usually go for these products and services?

These questions will not only provide you with important marketing information but help you establish an open communication line with the customer. They can also help your customers tell you what is important to them and let them know that you are sincerely interested in their specific and individualized needs.

Staying Focused On The Customer

Everyone talks about focus and keeping an eye on the ball; but what is the real, everyday focus of your business? Is your attention focused on marketing programs, payroll, a customer complaint, or is it on equipment, unpaid receivables, taxes, a troubled employee or how the work schedule isn't working? Maybe a personal problem is dominating your thoughts.

I can't tell you what specific issues need the most attention at your business, but I can tell you this—in day-to-day business operations, the issues that tend to get the most attention are problems that must be dealt with immediately. By virtue of something being a problem, it quickly becomes a priority. As it is often said, "the squeaky wheel gets the grease."

So how do you stay focused on the customer? First, realize that you will inevitably have problems and that those problems will cause you to occasionally redirect your focus and resources to fix them. Just accept them, deal with them and try not to waste more time on them than is absolutely necessary. Second, you can stay focused by not allowing the problems to become the overriding attitude of the day.

Here is a story about how easy it is to lose customer focus:

One afternoon, I stopped by a local deli to order a sandwich for lunch. As I entered, I noticed that the girl behind the counter was paying attention to a conversation between two other employees in the store (they were complaining about the schedule the shift manager had posted). I waited for her to greet me and ask for my order. After what must have been a full minute, she finally asked, without even looking at me, "What would you like?"

I was surprised at her disregard for me, but I ordered the sandwich anyway. Without saying a word or making any sort of affirmation, she just started making the sandwich. Every so often, she would look toward the other employees, but never at me. Being my normal, engaging self, I asked her how she was doing. She said "fine"—again, without looking up. After making my sandwich, she wrote the price on the wrapper and placed the sandwich on the counter without so much as another word to me—no eye contact, no "thank you." She just began to clean the counter.

I said nothing and took my sandwich to the cashier. I noticed that the man behind the counter was wearing a badge that read, "Customer Service Team Leader." I saw this as the perfect opportunity to share my poor experience with someone who would surely care; after all, that was his job—to lead the customer service team. I asked him if he would like to hear about my experience in his store. He said "Yes," so I proceeded to tell him about the girl's lack of interest and bad attitude.

I expected a comment from him that would convey an acknowledgement or an apology—something along the lines of, "We do appreciate your business, and we are always happy to see our customers." Instead he said, "We have been working since 4:30 this morning, and she is probably just tired." I replied in my nicest, most non-confrontational tone, "It doesn't take any more energy to be friendly, does it?" To my surprise, his answer was, "It has been a very busy day."

At that point, I realized he wasn't interested in making me feel better about the service, so I just said "thank you," paid and left. The sandwich was no longer the issue. This store's focus was obviously not on the customer but on letting the daily problems of the operations take over—even when it was brought to someone's attention. Was this the service standard the owners of this store had designed? All I know is that it was the standard I received on the day I was there. There are many other deli stores in that area, and I can assure you that I haven't been back to that one again.

My personal experiences visiting other businesses across the country are not much different. I'm sure many of you feel that there are countless examples of businesses that focus on excellent customer service. But the truth is that many employees don't see the customer as a person. They only view him as a transaction to be processed or, even worse, an interruption to their workday.

One day, a gentleman who was attending a workshop I was facilitating shared with me an interesting perspective. He said, "Customers don't care so much that you know, but they need to know that you care." I had not heard it said that way before, so I asked him to share more details. By "care," he meant having a staff that shows they are sincerely concerned if the customer has a problem or a question. Even when a staff member does not know the answer, an attitude of caring should be displayed by taking the time to find out the correct information and communicate it to the customer.

The number one reason a customer will stop patronizing a business is an attitude of indifference shown by an employee. It needs to be guarded against at all times when dealing with customers. Be aware, however, that indifference can be demonstrated at any time, by anyone; the employee could be a counter person, technician, the manager or, even worse, the owner of the business.

What makes matters more perplexing is that an attitude of indifference is not necessarily rooted in an overtly negative service attitude. Someone simply not being attentive, not stopping what they are doing while the customer is talking to her or appearing to be otherwise preoccupied can easily display indifference to a customer. In order to show an attentive attitude, you and your staff should always make eye contact with customers while conversing with them, occasionally nodding your head or using a word of acknowledgement to let them know that you are listening.

Chapter Six Summary

- Systems and processes control the experience
- People bring life to the systems
- Maintain operational excellence
- Learn to watch for the signs
- Recognize opportunities with your customers
- Stay focused on the customer

Customer Service Is A Contact Sport™

Chapter Seven

Maximizing Revenue Per Customer

All customers deserve the opportunity to purchase the products and services they need.

The main focus of this book is creating a business that excels at delivering excellent customer service and maximizes the opportunity to develop loyal customers. Delivering the highest level of service will no doubt go a long way toward assuring that your customers will return again and again. But maximizing the transaction dollar amount should be another priority. I am not suggesting you oversell customers. I am, however, suggesting you make sure each one has an opportunity to purchase the products he or she needs.

Increasing customer count is not the only way, and often not the best way, to increase revenue. For example, a friend of mine owned a small retail business that was not doing as well as it could have been. He blamed the mall for not advertising enough or the economic condition of his marketplace or his customers for not wanting to spend any money or the weather or the price of tea in China or just about anything else he could think of that he had no control over. However, having been a customer and friend of his for several years, I could see that these conditions were not the primary reasons for his limited success and that the solutions needed for success would involve some basic and fundamental changes to the way he thought about his business.

Wanting to help, I asked him: "Which area of your business would you most like to improve?" His answer came quickly and decisively: "Just bring me more customers." He didn't say, "I would like to improve customer service or my ability to properly train my employees so they can better serve our customers," and he didn't say, "I would like to improve the look and merchandising of my store." All he wanted was more customers. But what about all the customers he had already had who didn't go back to him? If he had focused on helping them purchase more of the products and services he offered, he would have been more successful financially.

As a consultant, I hear companies request more customers all the time, and I almost always look back to the customers they already had. Bringing more customers to a business that isn't taking care of the ones it already has only serves to process people through a business transaction. Unless the customer is developed properly, the simple fact that a transaction occurs does not assure he or she will ever return for future products or services.

Presenting The Opportunity

Customers cannot buy what they do not know you have for sale. Most retailers are not achieving their full revenue potential because they are not providing their customers with the opportunities to buy their full line of products. Many retailers are just happy to have the customer make a purchase of any amount. But even with a limited range of services and marginal technique, if a retailer and his staff are consistent in offering the customer the opportunity to buy, then revenues per customer will increase.

More often than not I find that businesses are not overselling but underselling. Customers are not being properly served if you don't give them the opportunity to purchase the products and services they need. Remember the purchase of my home audio system? As good as my salesman was, he still forgot to sell me a cable I needed for the installation. Sure, it only cost about $100.00, but if that happens a few times per week per employee, the revenues drop on a per-transaction basis.

Train your staff how to identify additional revenue opportunities and to properly present those needs to your customers—without exception. Also, train your employees how to let a customer say "yes" or "no" comfortably. It's not so much about sales as it is presentation of information.

Focus

People generally talk about what is important to them. When your staff hears you talk about speed of service being important, they work faster. When they hear you talk about excellence in customer service, they find ways to give it. When they hear you talk about completely providing for a customer's needs, they will identify and qualify those needs more willingly.

On the other hand, attaining higher revenue per customer is also an integrated process and has as much to do with the image of your business, the services and products you offer and the price and quality of those products as it does with how your customers feel about you and your employees. And just as with customer service, enhancing revenue per customer is a matter of where you focus your attention.

The process of increasing average revenue per customer can be broken down into three segments that will help you evaluate your current situation and focus on some foundational issues that will make implementation easier: range of products and services, presentation technique and consistency of presentation.

Range Of Products And Services

No matter how good a job you do of taking care of your customers' base needs, you will not maximize sales opportunities if you don't offer a full line of complementing services or products. Doing so accommodates the true needs of your customers—even the needs they don't know they have. Theoretically, you could reach a point where you offer too many services and lose both your focus and your core business. But I believe that offering a complete (within reasonable limits) range of services is better for your business and your customer.

Presentation Technique

Simply asking the customer if he wants a product is a good start and better than not asking at all, but there are more effective ways to approach someone who has a valid need. One of the most important techniques for increasing sales and improving service—which is also one of the easiest to teach—is presenting, not selling.

Imagine you are at a nice restaurant and after finishing your meal the server asks, "You want desert?" Most people would be inclined to say "no" to that kind of inquiry. Sure, at least the server asked, but how could the suggestion have been made in a way that would have enticed the customer to respond affirmatively? How could the dessert option have been made irresistible?

One highly effect technique for increasing the likelihood that a customer will buy dessert begins while the customers are still eating their meals. While checking to make sure everything is to the diners' satisfaction, the server should suggest that they save room since there are some delicious items on the dessert menu. Then, when the appropriate time comes to offer dessert, the customers should be presented with their options in the most appealing way. This is especially effective with desserts because they can be made to look so tempting. Using a dessert tray with samples of the menu items is visual and therefore more effective than merely telling the customer the choices. The combination of planting the thought of dessert in the customers' minds during their meal and showing them the selections in person will result in more customers purchasing this profitable add-on.

What are the "desserts" in your business? Maybe your additional products and services are not as appealing as a slice of gorgeous, triple-chocolate cake, but everything has its own appeal. Think about how you could present your additional items to your customers. Consider not only how but when in the sales transaction the best time to present them would be. Is there a preface statement that you could use early in the process that would prepare the customer and get him thinking about the additional items? When done properly, you will be surprised how many people will thank you for making the suggestion.

Consistency

Consistency is one of the most challenging aspects of increasing revenue per customer, but it yields the greatest return on the time spent to make it happen. It is as easy as always letting customers know about additional services or products and trying not to predetermine their willingness to purchase them. Give customers options; the more effective you are at presenting options and upgrades, the more often customers will say "yes."

Imagine if you were a home heating specialist, and your customer was required to replace a filter in the heating unit of her home. Failure to do so might result in less efficiency and damage to the unit. If you as the professional fail to advise the customer of this important maintenance item, have you helped or hurt her? You may occasionally get the customer who says, "Don't try to sell me anything; just give me what I asked for," and, of course, you must honor the request. But you still must do your job and advise her of anything else that might be needed. It's not an option—it's part of the job. I have never heard of anyone who got upset at a server for asking if she (the diner) would like coffee or pie after her dinner. If the suggestion is made properly, most men will not object to being shown a tie and shirt to go with a suit purchase. On the other hand, he may be less than satisfied if he gets home and realizes he doesn't have a tie to go with his new suit.

Making It Happen

All this talk about attaining additional revenue from existing customers sounds good, but what if you don't think your employees will do it? Maybe you've tried to get them to before and you just couldn't seem to make it happen. Let's look briefly at some of the obstacles you may need to address before you can get the results you are targeting.

Why Don't Your Employees Ask Customers If They Would Like To Purchase Additional Items?

There are numerous reasons: they don't believe in the service, they don't understand the value to the customer, they think the customer may be offended if they offer it, they think the customer can't afford it, they think the customer may say "no," they think the service is priced too high, they forget to ask or they just don't want to make the effort. Any one of these will result in the same outcome—reduced sales and customers who don't get the opportunity to purchase products or services that would benefit them.

Why Do Customers Resist Add-On Sales?

They may decline to purchase an additional item for many reasons, including: they don't think they need the service or product, they don't have the time, they don't have the money, they don't like the service they are receiving, they don't like the person serving them, and the list goes on and on.

How Can You Make Additional Sales Easier For Employees?

Effective systems and training help make the job of suggesting additional items to your customer easier and more productive. Proper compensation and supportive motivation also rank near the top of the list.

Proper presentation is not a guarantee that your customers will purchase additional items, but it will certainly improve the chances. If, at the very least, you offer the product or service, you will be doing the right thing for your customers and your business.

Doing The Right Thing

Now that we have reviewed some of the more important steps to increasing revenue per customer, how do you make sure it happens? How do you get your employees to do it? The short answer is "motivation." Everyone needs motivation—your employees, your customers and, yes, even you.

There are many different schools of thought on the subject of motivation, specifically when it pertains to consistently presenting additional products and services. Even though people have come up with all kinds of motivation and bonus programs, one of the most tried and true motivators is simply doing the right thing.

Being motivated to do the right thing would especially come into play if, while you were assisting one customer, the store was very busy and other customers were stacked up, waiting in line. At this point, it would be easier to just get your patron what she asked for and move on to the next customer. But what if she needs more than what she initially came in for? Again, doing the right thing should be the main focus. In this case, that would require sticking with the first customer and seeing that sales transaction through to the end.

And just as it's wrong to offer a customer a service that is not needed, not offering a product or service that *is* needed is also wrong. Customers generally come to your business to purchase something or take care of a need, so underselling is just as inappropriate as overselling. I have come across more businesses that undersell than oversell. Why? I think it is often because some businesses don't want to appear pushy, or maybe they have had customers tell them about other businesses in town they will never go back to because they tried to sell them something they didn't need.

Maximizing Revenue Per Customer

Sometimes, however, it can be hard to reconcile being motivated with doing the right thing. As we saw in Chapter Four, some people ask, "What's in it for me?" which has the potential to be a self-serving attitude, or motivation; and it can be, if applied in a selfish manner. But if you look closely enough, you will find a process of "give and take" at the root of almost every personal and professional relationship, whether it's employer-employee, customer-business or husband-wife. Employers want the job to be done right while employees want appreciation and fair compensation. Customers want the best value for their money while businesses want the customers to be loyal to them. Husbands want their wives to understand them, and wives want their husbands to listen to them. Most people are motivated at some level to do what others want if it means their own needs are being met as well. This doesn't mean that we're all necessarily self-serving; but if you listen to people closely enough and learn enough about them, you will usually discover what motivates them.

For instance, money can be a powerful motivator, but it can also motivate some people to do the wrong things for the wrong reasons. Some people will try to sell a customer something he doesn't need just to make a commission. You may get away with it once or twice, but eventually, the lack of integrity will lead to the business's demise. The customer will find out and stop patronizing it, which is precisely why many businesses that traditionally paid their employees based on commissions have moved away from that method. Lining one's pockets with money from services or products the customer doesn't need is the equivalent of stealing. People need to monitor their motivations against a moral standard other than how much money they can make from a customer.

Don't misunderstand me. Money is not the problem any more than it is the solution. Employees providing a professional service deserve to be paid well for what they do, and allowing compensation to be tied to performance is one of the best ways to reward good work. However, any time someone can personally gain by selling someone something, the opportunity and potential for abuse exist. Doing something because it is the right thing to do has a way of rewarding people in ways that money can't.

Doing the right thing affects every aspect of motivation in business, from motivating your staff to higher levels of service and customer satisfaction to motivating employees to take more care in the technical aspects of their jobs. I believe that motivation comes from several internal and external sources. I have seen some of the best service teams and companies achieve the highest levels of motivation without any additional money. Instead, motivation comes from external incentives like flextime, contests, awards and the most important incentive of all—the desire to support one's self and family, which is why people work in the first place. Finding these ways to motivate your employees is critical to achieving the highest number of happy customers and happy employees.

Chapter Seven Summary
- Give the customer the opportunity to purchase
- Talk about increasing revenue
- Inventory what your customer needs
- Present, don't sell
- Be consistent in offering to every customer
- Do the right thing

Chapter Eight

Complaints—A Gift From Your Customer

If customers never complained, you would never know what could be improved about your business.

Statistics indicate that eighty percent of customers will not complain openly. Instead, they will just take their business elsewhere and never tell you why. Now that is a scary thought. It is like your business is sick and no one will tell that it's sick or how it might get better.

Even when business is good, you could be losing customers and not even know it. As a matter of fact, one of the most difficult things I do as a consultant is try to estimate how much business a client is losing. Losing business can be caused by competition, unresolved complaints or any number of reasons. And while you will have a difficult time trying to control your competition and other external competitive factors, you *can* control, or at least have a major influence on, virtually everything that happens inside your store.

I often hear clients vent their frustrations about seemingly never being able to please their customers. They say their customers complain too much; they complain about what they don't have in stock or the fact that what is in stock is not what they want. They complain about prices, service, employees and on and on.

Customer Service Is A Contact Sport™

No one likes hearing negative comments about his business, but when you think about it, a complaint is really a gift—a gift of information a customer is giving to you that can improve your business. In fact, the vast majority of customers who do complain about something do so because they would like to see you improve on it so they can continue to be your customer. Most customers believe that you care and want to improve your business.

If you have customers, you will inevitably have customer complaints. It is a fact of life in a retail business. This chapter is focused on helping you to make the most of every complaint you receive, to treat them as gifts and to realize that each and every one contains the seeds of improvement.

If you have been in business for awhile, you have no doubt heard that if you please a customer she will tell one or two friends about your business, and then each of those people will, in turn, tell one or two friends and so forth. However, if you displease a customer, she will tell as many as ten of her friends. Why the large disparity between sharing good news and sharing bad news?

Customers rarely get emotional about good service, but they tend to get quite emotional about poor service. Think about the last time someone gave you poor service, or worse yet, gave you a hard time because you had a complaint. Depending on the severity of the situation, you may have become upset, and by nature, when people are upset, they tend to speak more readily and with more emotion and passion. That being said, how much more convincing is a customer when she tells a friend about her poor experience at your facility and that the friend should not patronize your business? Is this fair? No, but it is how most people react.

Why Are Some Customers Difficult?

Customers come to your business with many personal issues that have nothing to do with your and your business. Sometimes they come into your business with chips on their shoulders, ready to jump at the first person who crosses them. In such cases, a normally calm person can be provoked to anger and do and say things he would normally never say. Most customers do not complain because they want to ruin your day, although it may sometimes feel that way. Rather, they just want someone to hear their dilemmas and fix their problems.

Here are several reasons why customers might get the feeling they not being treated properly and therefore become difficult:

Some Customers Feel Ignored

This is one of the most frequent customer complaints. They are either deliberately ignored by employees, or they get the feeling they're being ignored because they cannot find someone to assist them. I recently observed a customer in a large hardware store, who stood in the middle of the aisle and literally yelled to an employee who was at least several aisles away, inquiring where a particular item was located. I am sure the employee thought this was unbelievably rude; in fact, it was. However, for you to understand the big picture in this situation, I should also tell you I had overheard the man speaking to his wife in the aisle next to me a few moments before, saying how frustrated he was getting not being able to find someone to answer his questions. Evidently, he had searched for several minutes before finally losing his composure.

Some Customers Have Been Taken Advantage Of In The Past

Most of us have been taken advantage of at some point in our lifetimes, so we all know what it feels like. Some customers are predisposed to be more difficult because they are protecting themselves against being taken advantage of again. It has nothing to do with you, but if you are in the same line of business as the culprit who took advantage of this customer previously, you will feel the normal skepticism of someone protecting his interests.

Some Customers Don't Feel That You Respect Them

Obviously, if you are taking care of your customers properly they will never feel this way at your store. However, a feeling of disrespect can arise quickly when an employee makes a customer wait while he finishes a personal telephone call or fails to make positive eye contact or sends other expressions or actions that signal to the customer that he doesn't appear to care.

Some Customers May Feel Embarrassed Or Insulted

They may feel this way because they don't know something they think they should know or because an employee is being condescending. When a customer appears to lack knowledge about a particular issue, that's the perfect opportunity to educate and inform him without talking down to him.

Owners and managers who ignore or mishandle customer complaints are missing out on the most important feedback their businesses can receive. Your customers are taking the time to tell you exactly how you need to improve your business in order to ensure their repeat business. What better gift could you receive?

Complaints should be viewed as an opportunity to improve a specific aspect of your business. Dealing with a customer complaint is much better than the customer never coming back, yet a large number of business owners are insulted by the suggestion that they're not running their businesses properly. Why? Somehow, they have failed to realize that even in the best of businesses, there's room for improvement. If a customer does complain, don't take it as a personal attack; look at it as someone taking the time to provide you with information you can use to make your business better. Thankfully, some customers do complain.

A friend of mine who works in a restaurant told me about a customer who came in with a complaint. The customer calmly approached the counter and said, "Every time we've been in this restaurant, we've not had good service. If it happens again, we won't be back." At this point, many employees would have just looked at the customer with their "What's your problem?" stare, which would have caused the customer to blow a gasket.

However, my friend, being very customer service-oriented, responded with a caring and helpful attitude. Instead of ignoring the comments, she took a personal interest in making sure the customer was going to be happy with this visit. First, she apologized and then asked what the previous problems had been. The man said that his meal wasn't what he had ordered and that the food wasn't fresh.

Again, my friend apologized, and as the customer ordered, she took extra time to make sure his order was correct and allowed him the opportunity to change his order as he saw fit. Then she took the customer's comments to the cooks, who prepared the man's meal, taking extra care to be sure that he received exactly what he ordered and that the food was hot and fresh. She delivered the meal to the customer and made sure to tell him that dessert would be on the house. The customer was skeptical but satisfied. As he ate his meal, my friend made sure to keep his drink filled and was available if the man needed anything else. These were all things that should have been done anyway, but in this case, they were done with extra care so she could save this customer's business.

When the customer was ready for dessert, my friend offered the selection and asked if she could serve him coffee. He accepted and enjoyed it with his dessert. Throughout the meal, my friend continued to check in with the man to see if he needed anything. She also brought the manager over and introduced him to the customer. The manager thanked the man for bringing his complaints to his attention and made sure the customer felt appreciated for doing so. The customer left the restaurant having received a good meal and feeling cared for in the process. He has returned to that restaurant many times since then.

Making The Most Of The Complaint Opportunity

All businesses need to know what customers think of them. Encourage your customers to communicate with you, and make it easy for them to comment or even complain. It can be as easy as placing a small sign near your counter that reads: "We care about your comments and suggestions. They help us improve our business. Please tell our manager about our service today—we hope it was to your satisfaction!"

When a customer makes a comment about your business or chooses to complain outright, you should receive this gift in such a way as to make the customer feel comfortable and positive about taking the time to give it. These seven steps will help you in the process:

1. Stop what you are doing
2. Apologize and offer to help
3. Listen actively and recap
4. Commit to action
5. Review all possible solutions
6. Thank the customer
7. Follow up

1. Stop What You Are Doing

Nothing will raise the customer's level of irritation more than someone who acts as though he doesn't care. Whatever else you are doing at the time, stop it, if possible. If you need to, ask the customer to give you a moment to finish what you are doing so you can give him or her your undivided attention.

2. Apologize And Offer To Help

First, apologize—not because you did something wrong but because the customer has a problem. Then offer to help. I have a saying that goes, "No one kicks holes in the bottom of the boat he's riding in." So get into the boat with your customer by offering your help. You might say something like, "Let me see if I can help you." You want the customer to see you as a potential advocate, not an adversary.

3. Listen Actively And Recap

All good communications start with someone being willing to listen. Don't try to defend your position; just listen. Allow your customer to speak without interruption. Keep good eye contact with him and acknowledge his comments with an occasional nod, if appropriate. Once the customer has an opportunity to express his comment, repeat it back to him in your own words. For example, if Mr. Green is upset because his dry cleaning came back with stains on it, you should repeat his complaint back to him: "So, you dropped the shirts off on Tuesday, and the only stains were on the cuffs, but now the pockets are stained. Is that right?" That shows that you're listening and that you understand the complaint properly and in its entirety. This also goes a long way to diffuse the customer's immediate feelings of anger.

4. Commit To Action

Once you have gathered information about the problem, you need to commit to providing a solution. Depending on the nature of the problem, it may be as easy as asking the customer what he would like you to do to make him satisfied. Oftentimes a customer will surprise you and tell you he wants only to let you know about the problem so you can fix it. Sometimes, you may be able to solve the complaint right on the spot. Other times, someone will ask for more than you can properly give, or you may need to look into the situation further. If that is the case, then take the customer's contact information and make a commitment to get back to him within a reasonable time. Usually twenty-four to forty-eight hours is sufficient for you to decide on a solution and get back to the customer.

5. Review All Possible Solutions

Take time to review the complaint, and once you have decided upon the appropriate resolution, take care of it; get it done and get back with the customer so you can let him know your course of action.

6. Thank The Customer

Don't forget that this customer gave you a gift—information that will help you run a better business and more than likely keep him as a customer.

7. Follow Up

If the nature of the complaint requires you to follow up, do so and do it promptly. Generally, a follow-up call or note should be sent within three to five business days.

Obviously, you can't put your business in a position to be taken advantage of by unscrupulous people who would like to pull one over on you. However, the percentage of people who will try to take advantage of you is quite small—perhaps only one percent. That means that ninety-nine percent of customers are sincere in their complaints and only want a resolution. Don't penalize the vast majority of your honest customers by not giving them the benefit of the doubt when they have complaints.

The vast majority of people will not take time to write a letter or fill out a form. Often, the only feedback you have to help you gauge how well or how poorly you are doing are subtle comments, gestures or facial expressions from the customer.

Knowing that a customer has a complaint is evident if he walks into your business and commands your attention. Sometimes, though, you need to be in the right place at the right time to see that there's a problem. To ensure your accessibility to customers with complaints, you can take the following proactive steps:

Be available to your customers. Be where the action is, and listen to what is going on around you. Learn to listen to more than one conversation at a time. Pay attention when you think you are hearing a complaint starting to arise. Watch for the signs of an unhappy customer.

When a regular customer has been to a competitor, ask her about her experience. This needs to be done subtly, but it does show you care.

Call on certain customers—the ones you think might have problems or the potential for problems—to make sure they are satisfied. To be even more positive, call on several customers at random, just to show you care about their patronage and the quality of your service.

Ask your employees for suggestions. They know a lot more about what your customers want and need than you sometimes give them credit for.

Monkeys On Your Back

Handling customer complaints can be difficult and time-consuming, but if it's done properly, it can reap big dividends for your business. From time to time, however, other complaints and problems will come to you as well that threaten to take time away from your customer service mission. Often they are brought to you by your employees.

If you have ever had an employee come to you to solve a problem, then you know the meaning of "having monkeys on your back" ("monkeys" referring to the problems, not the employees!). Often your staff members could figure out a solution for themselves, but it becomes easier for them to come to you for answers. After all, you are the boss.

This is an easy trap for anyone running a business to fall into. In the moment, it seems easier for you to solve the problem than to take the time to show your employees how to arrive at the appropriate solution on their own. But by repeatedly doing this, employees don't learn an effective problem-solving process, and they don't develop the confidence to work on their own. Thus, they will always feel the need to come to you.

Another problem with this approach is that you already have a full agenda with issues that demand your attention. Taking on other people's problems will ultimately overload you and keep you from getting your own agenda accomplished. In addition, you will have less time to focus on the most important issues in your business—taking care of your customers and training your employees.

Imagine this scenario: you are busy doing something on your "to-do" list, and one of your managers comes to you with a request to revise the bonus program. He tells you he needs to make more money and, in effect, hands you his "monkey." You take it, adding this bonus revision issue to your ever-growing list of things to do. You don't have the extra time, but you know this is an important issue, and you want to take care of a good manager.

Although you ultimately need to be involved in the final decision, a more effective response would be to have the manager make some suggestions to you for possible solutions, so you both can discuss them together at a later date. This approach will keep your manager from giving you his "monkey" and encourage him to come up with some viable options. Later, when you meet to discuss his suggestions, you can review them and walk him through the problem-solving process necessary for arriving at the best solution for him and for the company.

It is sometimes hard to let go of the control and let your employees solve problems. I know this first-hand because I struggle with this same challenge. It takes a conscious effort and a lot of patience to let people make some mistakes along the way. But this process is important and demonstrates to your staff that you trust them. To help you gain confidence throughout the process of letting go, start with small responsibilities, and once you feel certain about your employees' abilities, allow them to handle larger issues. You may want to establish limits on any issues that require a financial outlay from the company or materially affect company policies.

If your schedule is busy with projects that take you off site, then your commitment to teaching your employees to deal with their problems becomes even more critical. I remember visiting with the manager of a group of business facilities, who complained that he could never get the owner to sit down and listen to his suggestions or make a commitment to various issues. Upon further questioning, I discovered the real problem: the manager was bringing issues to the owner with the notion that the owner would come up with solutions himself.

The owner already had a full agenda of things to do and no spare time to solve the manager's issues, but because he was the owner, he felt compelled to do so. He would listen to the manager but then never get around to providing him with a solution. This only needed to happen a few times before the manager quit sharing ideas and stopped communicating altogether. The manager also began to think that the owner was not committed to the business. And if the owner didn't care, why should he?

A proactive response to this kind of situation is to encourage your employees to think through a few solutions for your consideration before you all mutually decide on the best one. You not only save time in the process, but the employees will take more ownership in the applied solution.

In the previous example, I also advised the manager to put his specific issues and suggestions in writing and to submit that list to the owner for his review and approval. I advised him to make sure there was a space for the date and the owner's initials, basically making it easy for the owner to respond to his requests.

Although you want to empower your employees, you need to stay aware of what is happening in your business and give your people guidelines for what you'd like to be apprised of immediately. Set specific guidelines for which types of problems employees should handle on their own and which they should share with you immediately or in the near future. For example, you may require your employees to report specific problems like accidents, or you may want to stay involved in all customer complaints. Setting these parameters allows you to stay on top of situations in which you should absolutely be involved.

As lack of time continues to be an issue in most of our professional lives, the possibility of empowering employees to handle different situations on their own becomes vital. Teaching employees how to competently solve problems and effectively manage conflicts that occur in your day-to-day business is a winning move for both you and your staff. You will gain useful time and creative suggestions for solving problems, and your employees will gain a sense of accomplishment because they are an important and valued part of your team.

Complaints—no one wants them, but everyone needs them. Whether they come from customers or employees, they can help you improve your business.

Chapter Eight Summary
- Complaints are gifts
- Difficult customers often have their reasons
- Make the most of the complaint opportunity
- Don't feed other people's monkeys
- Be proactive

Chapter Nine

Measurement And Management

You can't manage what you don't measure.

"You can't manage what you don't measure." When I first heard that statement many years ago, I almost couldn't grasp the beauty of its simplicity. The process of determining how any aspect of your business is performing must start with some objective measurements—not just feelings and instincts. In fact, you could go so far as to say that if something is important to your business, you will measure it; and conversely, if you don't measure it, it must not be important. But the reality is that many important things do not get measured in our businesses.

For example, is customer service important to your business? Do you objectively measure it, or do you just have a *feeling* that it is good or *sense* that it needs improvement? By objectively measuring any aspect of your business, you gain the information that you need to determine if what you are doing is producing the results you intended. You can have a sharp focus on a goal, but if you don't measure it, you don't really know what progress you are making towards attaining it. More specifically, if you don't measure your goals and objectives, you can't manage them.

First, it is important that your measurement methods be accurate in order for you to get a true picture of your performance. During a recent client visit, I found that his Point-

Customer Service Is A Contact Sport™

of-Sale computer system was reporting transaction intervals of seventeen to eighteen minutes, when in reality the transactions were taking much longer to be completed. After a more thorough analysis, I found that employees were pausing the system during the service process, which meant that the intervals were closer to twenty-five to thirty minutes. This was having a significantly negative impact on the number of customers serviced and on the customers who were waiting a long time for service. These people were not likely to purchase additional services that would keep them at the facility even longer.

If you are computerized, be sure that you are using all of the tools that are built into the system. Call your vendor and ask them to provide you with a current summary of the most useful reporting and tracking systems. You may be amazed at how much measurement power you have sitting on your counter that you are not utilizing.

Just A Little More Effort

Sometimes the difference between success and failure can be measured by the smallest of margins. For example, a sharpshooter in a tournament must hit the bull's-eye of the target more times than the competition. A competitor could get close all day long but still lose the competition by missing the target by a fraction of an inch. Close only counts in horseshoes.

Those of you who water ski might remember what it was like to be dragged behind the boat when you were first learning to get up on one ski. You were halfway out of the water, being pulled at thirty-five miles per hour, your mouth getting full of water and your arms getting tired. If you didn't get the ski up out of the water soon, you would either drown or let go. However, with just a deep breath and a little more effort, you got up on the ski, and once you were on top of the water, you found it was easy. You could experience the freedom of water skiing and understand what people liked about it. It is often a similar experience in business. If you are not up and out of the water (making money), it is not much fun and can be very tiring.

A client called me one day and told me he was considering selling his business because he had reached what he felt was his limit. He couldn't seem to make the business work the way he had planned, and it had just become no fun for him any longer. Based on his knowledge and skill levels at that time, he was right to consider selling. But with more knowledge regarding some specific solutions to a few problem issues and with the development of some management skills, he is now better able to handle the challenges that had been making him feel defeated. Instead of selling, he soon set about the task of expanding his business to more locations. He went from almost drowning, or letting go, to successfully skiing on top of the water. Quite a change!

If I told you that your challenges were "all in your head," you might think that I was out of touch with reality. However, many of the problems we face actually *are* in our heads. These situations are often made more difficult by the way we look at them. Call them paradigms, perceptions or whatever makes sense to you, but how you respond to any challenge or opportunity starts with how you look at it.

Game Improvement

When I first came up with the concept of customer service being a contact sport, it changed the way I communicated it to others. Most of us understand that football, basketball and soccer are contact sports, but to think of retail as a contact sport surprises many until they realize the planned contact that is involved and the preparation it takes to compete at the highest levels of the retail game.

The higher an athlete rises in his chosen sport, the more disciplined and focused he must be. Whether it's a team sport like football or baseball or an individual sport like golf or bowling, game improvement comes at a price.

Take golf, for example. One of the many things I love about it is that it is completely objective—constantly teaching me something new or reminding me of something I already know but am not doing. Golf and business are similar in many ways. Both games are totally objective. When the competition is over and the scorecard is tallied, you generally get what you've earned. The scorecard indicates how well you played the game, and it doesn't lie. If you play well, you'll score well. The occasional lucky shots may win a game once in a while, but you will never build a career in golf if you just rely on a few lucky shots.

Golf is easy to talk about but much harder to play. It always amazes me how many armchair golfers will watch the final round of a pro tournament and tell you exactly what the players should have done to win. Yet these same people usually have handicaps over 20, can't drive the ball more than 175 yards (much less the typical professional drive of more than 300 yards) and they might never have even competed in a local tournament. Likewise, customer service is easy to talk about but much harder to deliver on game day. And in retail, every day is game day.

What you know or don't know becomes obvious when you are on the course. You can dress the part and even talk a good game, but does the ball fly straight and true? Do your putts go in the hole in fewer strokes? If you do not know the game of golf, it will

Measurement And Management

be obvious by the results. The same is true of customer service. Dressing the part and knowing the right terms isn't enough.

To improve your game, whether it's on the golf course or behind the counter of your shop, practice these guidelines:

Learn The Game

Every game requires you to know the rules and acquire the skills needed to play well. In golf, you have to learn stance, grip, swing, driving, short and long iron play, putting and course management. In business, there are communication skills, employee selection and development, performance management, customer service, merchandising, marketing and business management. Just as in any sport in which you intend to excel, you must acquire the knowledge and develop your skills in business.

Also, how you feel about the game will determine what you do and how well you do it. Are you tired? Rushed? In a bad mood? In golf, how you feel affects not just your game but those playing with you. In your business, your attitude (or the attitudes of your employees) greatly affects everyone on the team, not to mention the customers you serve. Attitude determines altitude, and the same holds true for your employees.

Know Your Equipment

Your equipment influences your game, and how you use the equipment influences your results. In golf, this includes you, your clubs, the ball and the course. In retail, your equipment could be your store, the computer system, your products or virtually anything that helps you serve your customers.

Customer Service Is A Contact Sport™

Know The Course

In golf, the game is won by getting the ball from the tee into the hole in the fewest number of strokes. The more you know about the course you are playing on, the more effectively you can adjust your game—your swing, choice of clubs and game strategy—to score well. Even the weather can change the course conditions, requiring you to alter your game strategy and the shots you take.

In business, the game is won by getting customers to come in for the products and services you offer and continue to come back time after time. Customer service is probably the most important element of the retail business game. Product offerings change like the weather, and competition affects customer demand. The more you and your employees understand your customers and the marketplace, the better you will be able to serve them with excellence and keep them coming back.

Practice

In both golf and business, you have to practice your skills—or change them—in order to improve. You've no doubt heard the adage that "practice makes perfect." It's not entirely true. I know many golfers and people in business who have been playing/practicing for many years but are practicing bad technique. The result is they get good at executing a skill incorrectly and producing poor results. Only practicing the right skills the right way will produce the results you are looking for.

Strive For Consistency

We all hit good shots occasionally or have positive customer interactions, but the key to winning, both in business and on the course, is consistency. Can you deliver a great shot every time? Can you and your staff produce excellent customer service with every customer on every visit, regardless of the outside factors (weather, competition)?

Get Help If You Need It

Could your game be better? There are many ways to acquire the knowledge and skills you need to improve your golf game; reading a good instructional book, watching a golf video or even picking up pointers from friends who play better than you can be helpful. However, without knowing how you play, these sources provide you with limited information that could actually make your existing game worse. Anyone serious about making improvements on the links would do well to visit a golf pro. The best teaching pros understand how to evaluate your current game and help you to improve your results by building from your existing skill sets and helping you establish reasonable improvement goals. The same process applies if you are committed to improving your customer service game.

Have You Reached Your Potential?

One of the most challenging questions I am asked is, "How much more business do you think I could do?" In most cases, the answer is, "Significantly more than you are currently doing." However, the true potential of a business is linked to many variables, making it almost impossible to predict the potential for improvement.

In sports, especially in a game like golf, it is easy to compare one's performance against the pros playing at the same course. Given similar playing conditions, if a top pro shoots eight under

Customer Service Is A Contact Sport™

par for eighteen holes, one can measure a game against that and see what the potential for the game really is.

What about in your business? What could a touring pro (business pro) score in your area of retail? What RPC (revenue per customer) could he score? Given the same facility, the same employees and the same customers, could he score more than you? Just imagine holding your local course record at one under par. Sure, that score might stand up to the local competition, but what about the top pros? Could they shoot eight under? Ten under?

Do you know the true potential of your business? Have you reached it? How do you know? How do you know the revenue per customer you are generating is at full potential? Is it eighty, seventy or just sixty percent of the potential? It's always difficult to judge what you are missing.

In golf, the handicap system is an objective standard of measurement to which your score is compared. The problem in business is that many owners are unaware of the true potential of their businesses until they learn about some new strategy or technique and then try it out. Don't judge the potential of your business only by the standard of your current performance. Have someone come to play your "course." It could be helpful and would more than likely show you some areas of potential for your business. Hire someone you know who is successful in your particular business to come and spend a day or an afternoon on your course. Be careful, however, not to pick up bad habits or techniques from someone who does not bring anything positive to your game. Most people have opinions; few can translate them into processes that produce better results for you and your business.

Pros put their pants on the same way you and I do—one leg at a time. So what's the difference when it comes to their success? How do they achieve such outstanding results? In a sport, there is the obvious and significant advantage of a physical skill or gifts that allow the athletes to perform at higher physical levels. In business, however, that physical difference is not applicable. So to succeed in its chosen game, the professional organization must rely on other strategies.

You Don't Know What You Don't Know

One of the greatest challenges that stands in the way of improvement, whether it's a skill or a business practice, is first admitting you don't know what you don't know. In fact, you *can't* know what you don't know. You may have a feeling that something is missing, something that you sense should be there, but you just don't know what it is. For example, if someone asked you to split an atom, would you even know where to begin? I know I wouldn't. Of course, splitting an atom and running a successful business aren't the same, but I think you get the picture. If you don't have knowledge of something, you cannot easily accomplish it. Often, business owners are afraid to admit that they don't know something they think they should, so they just go on as if they do know everything. The problem is that this behavior robs them of the opportunity to improve.

One Plus One Equals Three

Don't go it alone. There is an infinite number of resources available to help you improve your business. Combining your knowledge and thoughts with another's to think through situations and come up with ideas that neither would have come

Customer Service Is A Contact Sport™

up with on his own is called synergy. This is one of the most underutilized resources among most business owners. Gathering people together for the sole purpose of brainstorming is used in many business circles and think tanks to solve all kinds of problems. The dynamic created when two or more people get together to create solutions is very powerful and almost impossible to achieve using other methods.

I want to close this book with a challenge: Expand your vision of customer service, and continuously improve the process not just of how you handle and develop customers but how you merchandise your business and how you train your employees and therefore enable them to help you attain this vision.

You see, I am an optimist. I believe that we can have a better world. I see it happening in different parts of the globe every day—in small towns and big cities—people being more respectful to each other, people holding doors open for each other and people saying "thank you."

I also believe that as professional retailers we are in a great position to affect how people interact with each other. And interact we do. The average person in the United States is a customer between five and seven times per day. Through improving customer service, we can set a higher standard in our businesses, with our employees and ultimately with our customers.

My hope is that reading this book has given you a new or refreshed perspective on something I feel is vitally important not only to our businesses but to our society as a whole. If the suggestions and concepts contained in this book can help retailers be more successful in business, they can also have an impact on their personal lives. You see, customer service really is a contact sport.

CRUSH IT

THE LEGAL NURSE BLUEPRINT FOR SUCCESS

JANICE DOLNICK BSN, RN, LNC

Copyright © 2019
Janice Dolnick BSN, RN, LNC
Crush It
The Legal Nurse Blueprint For Success
All rights reserved.

No part of this publication may be reproduced, distributed, or transmitted in any form or by any means, including photocopying, recording, or other electronic or mechanical methods, without the prior written permission of the publisher, except in the case of brief quotations embodied in critical reviews and certain other non-commercial uses permitted by copyright law.

Janice Dolnick BSN, RN, LNC

Printed in the United States of America
First Printing 2019
First Edition 2019

10 9 8 7 6 5 4 3 2 1

I DEDICATE THIS BOOK TO MY FELLOW NURSES WHO
ARE THE BACKBONE OF HOSPITALS, CLINICS, DOCTORS'
OFFICES AND CARE FACILITIES ALL OVER THE WORLD.
THANK YOU FOR ALL THAT YOU DO.

TABLE OF CONTENTS

CHAPTER ONE 1

YOUR WORK EXPERIENCE, REDEFINED

CHAPTER TWO 15

TRAINING AND GETTING ORGANIZED

CHAPTER THREE 23

POSITIONING YOURSELF PROFESSIONALLY

CHAPTER FOUR 37

CRAFTING YOUR ONLINE PRESENCE

CHAPTER FIVE 45

CREATING THE PERFECT WEBSITE

CHAPTER SIX 57

BLOGGING YOUR HEART OUT!

CHAPTER SEVEN 63

EMAIL MARKETING

CHAPTER EIGHT 75

THE POWER OF THOUGHT LEADERSHIP

CHAPTER NINE 81

NETWORKING IN THE REAL WORLD

CHAPTER TEN 91

NEVER STOP PROSPECTING

CHAPTER ONE
YOUR WORK EXPERIENCE, REDEFINED

Leaping Head-First into the World of Legal Nurse Consulting

Clocking in at the hospital that day, all I could think of was resting. I had driven two hours in the dark. The lukewarm coffee I chugged on my way through the parking lot wasn't having much of an impact. My eyelids felt like bricks. I was drowning in exhaustion.

This wasn't just sleepiness. This was burnout.

I was a veteran nurse with a decade of experience under my belt, and plenty of practice fighting off fatigue. I genuinely loved my job. I had worked hard to get there, and while working as an RN in a variety of settings, it had been my dream for years to work in a hospital. From a bird's-eye view, I was at the pinnacle of my career.

So why was the pit in my stomach getting heavier and harder to ignore as the months flew by? I began to wonder if there was anything in store for me besides more work and longer hours. Would I ever know what life was like outside the demands of my job? Would I ever have the chance to start a family? If I did, would I have the time and energy to be a good mom?

~ 1 ~

Just before entering the hospital that dim morning, I finally admitted something I'd been ignoring and avoiding for too long: nursing would take up as much time and energy as I let it. To live the life I wanted, I would have to find some different ways of pursuing the career I love.

You can probably relate. You're likely a registered nurse with at least a few years of experience under your belt, a deep love of your job, and a creeping fear of burnout. You can't imagine leaving the medical community, but you also know that you can't keep going at your current pace.

I wrote this book to show you that there is indeed another path forward. Your experience as a nurse is valuable beyond nursing itself. It is particularly valuable to the legal community. Establishing yourself as a legal nurse consultant will allow you to keep one foot in the medical world while starting to live life on your own terms.

My career as an independent LNC started with a lot of trial and error. It culminated in 2009, when I founded my own LNC company, National Nurse Consulting. This book is the blueprint I was so desperately looking for all those years ago.

WHAT IS A LEGAL NURSE CONSULTANT?

Legal nurse consulting is a growing industry of experienced nurses who trade their scrubs for suits and lend their unique expertise to the legal community. Legal nurse consultants, or LNCs, are hired by attorneys who need advice on medically-focused cases, and work alongside legal teams in a professional relationship.

CRUSH IT: THE LEGAL NURSE BLUEPRINT FOR SUCCESS

Your knowledge of the medical system is extremely valuable to legal professionals. How great is that? By working together, you can help attorneys and other legal professionals save time and money when they're working on cases that involve medical records of any kind.

Legal nurse consulting is often a revelation to registered nurses who have spent their careers focused intently on a single path. Who would have thought that you could step away from the hospital and instead work from anywhere at any time for a variety of interesting clients and cases?

It's time to take the professional blinders off, blink a few times, and look around. Legal nurse consulting is an established and growing field, and a lucrative one at that.

But don't quit your day job just yet: you still have a lot to learn. No one becomes a legal nurse consultant overnight, but you can, and you will if you're ready to put in the time and energy required to learn how it all works.

From this point forward, I want you to stop picturing yourself as an employee and start thinking of yourself as an entrepreneur. This mindset will be critical as you start to learn and build your own LNC business.

The first few steps will be tough, but the process is worth the early effort. Once you've established yourself, you'll be able to work from nearly anywhere, and you'll get to choose when to pursue new business and when to lighten your work schedule.

Before you gain your first client as an LNC, your nursing experience will be your only calling card. Attorneys are looking to partner with registered

~ 3 ~

nurses with significant experience in the field: to put it bluntly, you are only as valuable as the advice and insights you can bring to the table. If you're considering becoming an independent LNC, you should already have gained significant experience working in more than one medical specialty, and should be able to demonstrate expertise in your field.

If you're not there yet, that's okay. Keep growing and expanding your repertoire as a medical professional. It's a necessary part of the process, and I'll be here for you when you're ready.

But if you've got at least five years of experience as a practicing registered nurse, keep reading. I wrote this book for you.

AREAS OF PRACTICE

There are over one million lawyers in the United States. Not all of them try cases, and not all legal cases are medical-related. But a great many cases can benefit from your knowledge and experience as a nurse.

Getting Started in Legal Nurse Consulting: An Introduction to the Specialty, published by the American Association for Legal Nurse Consultants (AALNC), provides the following list of specialties that benefit especially from the input of LNCs:

- Medical malpractice
- Worker's compensation
- Personal injury
- Case management
- Billing fraud

CRUSH IT: THE LEGAL NURSE BLUEPRINT FOR SUCCESS

- Social security disability
- Life care planning
- Product liability
- Corporate and regulatory compliance
- Toxic torts (or injury cases involving hazardous substances such as pesticides; a "tort" is a civil wrong)
- Risk management
- Healthcare licensure investigation

WHY BECOME A LEGAL NURSE CONSULTANT?

Working as a registered nurse in a traditional setting is stressful. Doctors are often too busy to be polite. Patients need your undivided care and attention, and don't always call for it in the most considerate terms. You're on your feet every shift, and finding time for a quick bite to eat can feel like a job in and of itself. I get it. I've been there and I remember those days very clearly.

It isn't unusual for nurses to feel overworked and underappreciated. From our very first shift we realize this is par for the course. Fortunately, I can tell you that the pace is less hectic and the pleasantries flow more easily when you're a legal nurse consultant.

As a legal nurse consultant, be prepared for entirely new work environments. You'll primarily be working from home, at a courthouse, or at a law firm. If you're anything like me, there will always be a part of you that misses the excitement and chaos of an emergency room, but your work as an LNC can give you a similar rush of excitement and you can

still save lives, just in a different way. Your hard work behind the scenes and your testimony in court has the potential to determine someone's fate, granting them freedom or denying it.

For many nurses, becoming a legal nurse consultant is the beginning of living life on their own terms. The pressure is still on, and the stakes are still high, but in a different and often more manageable way.

IF EVERYONE'S DOING IT, WHY SHOULD I?

"Isn't everyone becoming a legal nurse these days?"

"What can I possibly bring to the table that doesn't exist already?"

It's true that legal nurse consulting is a fast-growing industry. But here's the bottom line: there are plenty of attorneys, clients, and cases to go around. The job possibilities are all but endless if you're willing to hustle, stay focused, and prove your value.

If you're still on the fence, please keep reading. I know that once you finish this book, you'll feel encouraged to follow your dreams no matter how steep the learning curve it may be.

If you want to change your life, you need to commit to a plan and follow through on it. Now's the time to make that commitment. Pledge to yourself right now that this is something you want. As soon as I set my mind on becoming a legal nurse consultant, everything began to fall into place.

ATTORNEYS WANT TO HIRE YOU—THEY JUST DON'T KNOW IT YET

Since legal nurse consulting is relatively young industry, many attorneys are not even aware of how useful and important your work can be. In fact, some attorneys still don't even know what a legal nurse consultant is.

A decade ago, when I launched National Nurse Consulting, most attorneys I contacted had never heard of legal nursing. At networking events, I would be met with blank stares as I explained to attorneys that I was a legal nurse consultant. The response was often positive enough, but too often ended with "I don't do medical malpractice cases."

I now use moments like those as an opportunity to educate attorneys on the value of LNCs. If medical records are involved in a case—which they are in a surprising range of situations—we LNCs can probably be of service.

Here's the real reason attorneys love LNCs: we're just as knowledgeable as medical doctors on matters pertinent to most cases, and much more cost-effective. While testimony in court from an MD is sometimes necessary, in most cases hiring a legal nurse consultant is a better use of an attorney's money and resources.

Once attorneys understand this, they will see your value.

GETTING PAID AS A LEGAL NURSE CONSULTANT

I know what you're thinking: how much money do legal nurse consultants make? Can you still make ends meet?

The answer is yes, especially once you become established and begin to earn repeat clients. The more clients you get on your books, the more money you can make, simple as that.

Your hourly rate and retainer fee may vary depending on how many years you've been practicing as an RN, your location, and the size of the caseloads you work on.

One of the main benefits of being an independent contractor rather than a full- or part-time employee is that you get to name your rate. You can charge by the case or by the hour. It's now up to you.

While we're talking about money, here's a tip: don't rely on discounts and special deals. This starts a landslide of price competition and lowers the value of the service you're providing.

While you may be able to draw new clients by offering first-time discounts, the inevitable price jump will likely make them flinch when it comes time to consider hiring you again. Even a moderate discount tells your clients to value you less. If you insist on charging full price every time, you will be more valued and appreciated as a professional.

Setting your rates can be tricky. Do some market research online about the average fees charged by LNCs in the state or province where your clients will be based. An attorney practicing in California or New York will likely be bringing in bigger bucks than one based in Wyoming or Montana.

The bottom line is that you absolutely must do your research! Do not skip this step.

CRUSH IT: THE LEGAL NURSE BLUEPRINT FOR SUCCESS

As a rule of thumb, the more money an attorney or law firm makes on a case, the greater the earning potential for you as a legal nurse consultant. A firm of more than fifty attorneys working on a class action will typically have set aside a bigger budget for your services than a solo attorney working on a small personal-injury case.

That said, it is completely realistic in many markets to charge upwards of $150 an hour.

Once you have a sense of the going rate in your market, aim high but be realistic. Attorneys are negotiators. Asking for too little will set the bar too low and present a poor impression of your abilities, and may cause problems in the future. Asking for well beyond the industry's average will earn you an automatic "no". You're an entrepreneur now: negotiating is part of the game.

Decide what your rate is going to be and remain firm about that number. Have a bottom-line rate that you're not willing to go below. Keep in mind that as an entrepreneur and independent contractor, you'll be paying more taxes and doing more administrative work (such as setting up and maintaining your business) than you were when you worked at the hospital. It makes sense to charge more than you might feel comfortable asking for at first: you're in a totally new industry, after all.

I often suggest that new LNCs get some formal accounting or personal-finance training. This can be a difficult skill to add, but since you'll be your own boss from this point forward, it's a crucial one.

~ 9 ~

Since implementing a fee schedule for my own business, I have never had anyone scoff at my rate. In fact, most attorneys comment on how much more affordable a nurse is over a medical doctor, and how much more help and information they receive for their money.

As an entrepreneur, you cannot compete based on price alone. There will always be someone to undercut you. Instead, focus on bringing the greatest possible value to your clients and on building strong relationships. People are more likely to buy from those whom they know, like, and trust.

THE REALITIES OF ENTREPRENEURSHIP

Being an entrepreneur is not for everyone. Before you dive in to this new endeavor, consider whether you're truly ready to work for yourself. Test the waters a bit. See if you can find some hours during your work week to create a business plan, connect with attorneys in your network, or subcontract your services to an existing LNC business. It will be hard to achieve success as an LNC if you hate what you do, so give yourself time to dip your toe in and see if it's the right fit.

You don't have to go all-in straight out of the gate, but switching careers is a big commitment and things will get very real very fast once you quit your job and become a full-time legal nurse consultant and entrepreneur.

Weigh out the pros and cons. If entrepreneurship and freedom is what you want, there *will* be sacrifices to make and risks to take. This is true for all of us former RNs now working as full-time LNCs.

CRUSH IT: THE LEGAL NURSE BLUEPRINT FOR SUCCESS

The benefits of running your own business are obvious, but like anything worthwhile in life, there will be ups and downs and you need to be prepared to stay the course when things get rocky.

When you become a legal nurse consultant, you will be leaving behind that sense of security that comes from collecting a regular paycheck and group benefits like health insurance and retirement plans. You need to consider how this will affect your finances and your family.

Then imagine the sense of freedom you will feel when you do take the leap and land your first client.

Not every personality is suited to building a successful legal nurse consulting business. Being an LNC requires compassion, organizational skills, the ability to think quickly and overcome obstacles, a strong work ethic, the desire to work long hours, psychological and emotional stability, the ability to communicate clearly and concisely, adaptability, a knack for problem-solving, and excellent attention to detail. If you check all these boxes, you're well on your way, and I do believe this industry would be a great fit for you.

Another vital element of becoming an entrepreneur is marketing. Once you launch your own business, you're no longer just an RN: you're now a marketer and a public-facing professional as well. You'll need a good supply of confidence to promote yourself and your business. That same confidence will come into play if you are asked to appear as an expert witness in court.

~ 11 ~

If you naturally have an outgoing manner, can maintain your composure under pressure, don't shy away from public speaking, and are able to form relationships easily, these traits will all work to your advantage as a legal nurse consulting entrepreneur.

READY TO GET STARTED?

If you have decided that starting an LNC business is for you, now is the time to commit to doing it right.

There are many things to consider when starting any new business. One key to a successful launch is leveraging whatever resources are available to you during the planning stage. Whether you are a novice entrepreneur or you've had some experience in this area, consider visiting a small business development center (SBDC) in your area to see what they have to offer.

Business licensing, regulations, and other requirements and restrictions vary from state to state, province to province, and county to county. This is where your local SBDC can really help guide you when you begin setting up your business.

Most communities have an SBDC branch that offers free business advising services. To find an office near you in the US, visit: https://americassbdc.org/small-business-consulting-and-training/find-your-sbdc/; to find one in Canada, visit: https://www.ic.gc.ca/eic/site/csbfp-pfpec.nsf/eng/la03285.html.

CRUSH IT: THE LEGAL NURSE BLUEPRINT FOR SUCCESS

These centers employ professional consultants who can advise you on the details of writing a business plan, bringing your idea to market, and expanding your business. They offer one-on-one counseling and training sessions to entrepreneurs in subjects ranging from business planning and marketing to accounting and financing.

CHAPTER TWO
TRAINING AND GETTING ORGANIZED

"By failing to prepare, you're preparing to fail."
— Benjamin Franklin

Certification as an LNC is a mid-career goal that reflects your successful experience: it is not a requisite for entry into the field. Still, it's wise to decide early on whether you'll pursue formal certification.

Legal nurse consulting occupies a space between two professions that rely heavily on professional certification, but does not itself require a license or any other credential of your skills. That's not to say that you can jump right in: legal nurse consulting does require some education on the specific needs of attorneys.

I recommend exploring the many different programs and peer support options available to you before making an informed, confident decision on how to prepare for a career as a legal nurse consultant.

Whether or not you decide to pursue formal certification, I recommend highly that you find a great mentor. An experienced mentor can help launch your business, and can continue to advise you as your business grows.

As the old saying goes, it takes a village: attempting to switch careers without any sort of guidance will only lead to frustration and failure. You have a lot to learn—more than you know at this point—and a mentor can help you avoid common pitfalls.

In case you're struggling to find the right person, I offer a structured mentorship and training program that might interest you. Check out my NNC Members Lounge [nnc-members.com] for more information.

If you choose to pursue formal certification, multiple avenues are available to you. The AALNC has a lot of great continuing education resources and training opportunities: some of these are free, but others cost money.

Not all training opportunities lead to certification, and some are of dubious value. Wendie Howland of TheExpertInstitute.com, legal nurse consultant and editor of the *Journal of Legal Nurse Consulting*, has this to say on the matter:

There are several commercial companies that advertise courses of study to prepare nurses for LNC work. They are very pricey, and offer certificates, not certifications, with several different sets of designations. The American Association of Legal Nurse Consultants offers a very cost-effective online course that prepares an aspiring RN for the LNCC certification, the only nursing certification in legal nurse consulting approved by the Accrediting Board for Specialty Nursing Certification.

CRUSH IT: THE LEGAL NURSE BLUEPRINT FOR SUCCESS

LNC CERTIFICATION THROUGH THE AALNC

To earn the Legal Nurse Consultant Certified (LNCC®) credential, you must take the LNCC examination. The exam itself takes approximately four hours and focuses on medical malpractice, personal injury and other areas of the law. It includes 200 multiple choice questions that address hypothetical case studies.

The LNCC exam is computer-based and is offered in the spring and fall of each year at test sites in most US states and Puerto Rico.

To be eligible to take the LNCC exam, you must have:

- current licensure as a registered nurse
- at least five years of experience practicing as an RN
- evidence of 2,000 hours of legal nurse consulting experience within the past five years.

As with most tests, you'll benefit greatly from taking the time to study first. According to LNCC.AALNC.org, the LNCC exam assesses your abilities as a nurse to:

- Educate yourself and your attorney clients on medical details of the case
- Ease communication among clients, experts, and other people
- Collect and investigate medical records
- Analyze the data in medical records
- Collaborate with attorney clients
- Draft medical materials that will be used as evidence in court

~ 17 ~

- Testify in court as an expert

The AALNC offers a review course designed to prepare you for the LNCC exam. The course is built around eleven pre-recorded webinar modules of about ninety minutes each, and draws from a book called the *3rd Edition of Legal Nurse Consulting: Principles & Practice*, which is available for separate purchase. More information is available at AALNC.org.

GETTING ORGANIZED

Getting certified as an LNC is optional, but becoming a master of self-organization is not.

All successful business ventures are built on repeatable, reliable systems and processes. For LNCs, this means a formal approach to paperwork. LNCs work with large amounts of documentation, and your marketing and invoicing efforts will generate even more paperwork. To stay on top of your work and maintain a high level of quality and consistency, you'll need to organize your documentation in a way that ensures that everything's at hand and nothing's in the way.

The goal of any document-organization system should be to produce exactly the right document in less than a minute: that's the level of responsiveness attorneys expect when they contact you. A file cabinet full of clearly labeled, color-coded file folders organized by type, year, and case name is a good start.

My personal office file cabinet is divided into four main sections:

- Invoices and retainer contracts
- Client information (names, contact information, and areas of specialty for each attorney or firm with whom I've worked)
- Case-specific information
- Medical research materials (for example, frequently used or difficult-to-find statistics)

Over time, you can add new categories and sub-categories that reflect the sort of work you do. Some LNCs find that filing documents by case number works best; others prefer to start with alphabetized folders devoted to each client.

A disorganized office impairs your work as an LNC. Your invoices, retainer contracts, and work product can easily get lost in the jumble. Attorneys literally don't have time for that. Clients need to feel confident that they're working with an LNC who takes the job seriously, and that means taking time every week to focus on the administrative and organizational side of your business.

I've emphasized invoicing a couple of times in this section, and for good reason: if you don't bill your attorney clients in a timely manner, they won't pay you. It's as simple as that.

When I first started out as an LNC, I was so excited to have clients that I focused all my time on getting the work done and let the organizational side of things slide. It took me *two years* to get paid by one of my clients! That wasn't my client's fault. It was mine alone.

Please learn from my mistakes. Take at least one full day a week to organize your office until you're sure that you have exactly what you need, exactly when you need it.

Digital documents stored on your computer should be organized in a way that matches your paper-filing system. Many of my attorney clients hire me more than once, so I store their invoices and other pertinent information in a separate file on my desktop for easy access. Within each folder, you'll probably find it best to sort files according to the client's name or the date on which each document was last accessed.

Before you accept your first client, invest in a service or device to back up your computer's files and store them off-site in case disaster strikes. If that seems like overkill, remember that your clients back up every bit of data pertaining to their practices. Trouble does sometimes strike, and when it does, your clients will expect you to have taken the same precautions they have.

Much of your time as LNC will be spent working from an office, whether at home, at a client's office, or in a coworking space. But the job can also call on you to serve as an expert witness in court.

Before you launch your own business, it helps to get acquainted with your new work environment. If you're working at home, set up your office intentionally and spend some long stretches there even before you take on your first client, to make sure you have everything you need.

The same goes for courtroom appearances. All new legal nurse consultants should attend a few depositions **before** they are asked to be expert

CRUSH IT: THE LEGAL NURSE BLUEPRINT FOR SUCCESS

witnesses. Reach out to your professional network and see if you can connect with an attorney directly to ask about attending a deposition. This will give you a chance to see how the process works *before* you're deposed as an expert witness, which should take away some of the nervousness you might have about this very public side of the business.

MAINTAINING A POSITIVE MINDSET AND BUILDING A SUPPORTIVE NETWORK

Imagine hitting the snooze bar at 6 a.m. on a Monday morning instead of trying to talk yourself onto your feet. That sort of freedom is exhilarating at first for new LNCs. But there's another side to the coin: freelance work can also feel scary and lonely at times, and it produces its own types of stress. So how do you maintain a positive attitude and clear frame of mind?

When you're just getting started, you'll be focused on hustling as hard as you can to land your first case, build some momentum, and start establishing a track record. But you should also take time to connect with other legal nurses who have walked the path on which you've just begun. Having like-minded peers to speak with on a daily or weekly basis is incredibly important for longevity in this business, both for emotional support and for practical guidance. Your network is truly critical to your success.

You may find a local group of fellow entrepreneurs that meet monthly at a local coffee shop. You may want to join a coworking space. You might even find other LNCs online. I run a private Facebook group for those that join my NNC Members Lounge [nnc-members.com] that facilitates

~ 21 ~

opportunities for LNC entrepreneurs to connect with one another. In my group, we share leads for new business opportunities, ask each other's advice on casework, and even just check-in with each other to make sure all is well.

It's much easier to stay optimistic when you feel emotionally supported and connected throughout this journey. Make a point of finding and joining a community as you begin your entrepreneurial journey, and continue to nourish those professional bonds. When things get interesting, and they will, a solid network really makes all the difference.

CHAPTER THREE
POSITIONING YOURSELF PROFESSIONALLY

It's all in the details

As an LNC, your medical opinion matters. Your curriculum vita, also known as your CV or resume, and a letter of introduction will showcase your medical expertise to potential clients. Just as prospective employers did when you applied for nursing jobs, potential attorney clients will want to review your CV before they consider hiring you.

If you're planning to rock it as a legal nurse consultant, you need to start thinking like a business owner. You also need to consider how you will position and market your business in a professional and unique way. You're no longer an employee, you're now an entrepreneur. Every business needs its own unique brand that helps it stand out in the marketplace.

In this chapter, I'll show you how to create a winning CV and a letter of introduction that will translate your work as a nurse into the qualities that attorneys look for in legal nurse consultants. I'll also guide you through a few baby steps to start creating a professional brand for your business.

~ 23 ~

DETAILS MATTER

Even if you have decades more experience than other RNs, your CV will not stand out unless it's professionally presented and includes all the right information. As nurses, we're trained to be detail-oriented. Legal nurse consulting is no different: just as at the hospital, details matter.

Your CV is your first chance to show potential attorney clients that you care about the details of their cases as much as they do. Make sure that every word is written and presented with intention.

BUILDING A SUCCESSFUL CV

In the previous chapter, we spoke about connecting with other LNCs and building a professional community. Now is a good time to ask a trusted and successful LNC friend if you can peek at their CV. This will give you an idea of what information you should include in your own CV, and how to present it. If you're at a loss for who to ask, you can also often find other LNC CVs through a simple google search or by using LinkedIn. Check out any job postings that law firms have posted for in-house legal nurse consultants. What are they looking for? What skills and experience do you have that overlaps their requirements? This simple bit of research can make a world of difference.

At all times, consider how you compare to the competition. Assuming you already have a CV geared toward your nursing career, you will now need to adapt that to your work as an LNC. Your history as a nurse and medical expertise is important: that's why attorneys need you!

~ 24 ~

Where have you worked? What did you do? What formal education do you have? What have been your most notable achievements? What specific skills and proficiencies do you offer?

Make sure to highlight all relevant legal nursing experience, and courses you have completed or certifications that you've earned. Include specializations and qualifications that distinguish you and present you as an asset to attorneys working on different kinds of cases.

Your CV should address more than just your career and education. You can also include information about internships, apprenticeships, certifications, teaching experience, or pro bono work. At the same time, make sure that your CV focuses solely on what you have accomplished in the medical and legal fields. To an attorney looking to make a quick hiring decision, anything else is just time-wasting filler.

You might want add a mission statement or a summary of qualifications that defines your unique selling proposition (USP), or what makes you uniquely positioned to assist attorneys as an LNC.

While most attorneys will want to speak to your references, it's common practice to leave those details off your CV itself, and instead to state "references available by request" at the end. If you have a long list of references and/or testimonials that you feel very confident in, you can include them in a separate document for distribution when you pitch your services directly to attorneys.

~ 25 ~

Alternatively, you can create a testimonials page on your website and include its URL on your CV (we'll cover your online presence in Chapter 5).

If at all possible, be ready to provide a reference from your supervisor at the last hospital you worked at as an RN (especially if you're a new LNC), or a glowing review from the last attorney you worked for (if you're a more experienced LNC).

Don't forget to ask your previous supervisors and clients if they would be willing to vouch for you. Negative feedback can derail your LNC business, so never assume what someone might say about you. Approach each potential reference first and ask for their blessing to share their information with prospective clients.

Once you've assembled your CV, review it critically. Are there any spelling or grammatical errors? Are you getting straight to the point? Are you providing measurable proof of your expertise? Is there anything you included that an attorney would consider irrelevant when selecting an LNC? Edit your CV, and then edit some more!

Design is another aspect of your CV to bear closely in mind. Here are some simple guidelines to ensure that your CV looks professional and draws attention for only the right reasons:

- Consider the overall look and feel of the document. What does your CV document say to you before you even read a word of the text?
- Use a simple, readable, and consistent font.

~ 26 ~

CRUSH IT: THE LEGAL NURSE BLUEPRINT FOR SUCCESS

- Choose black or dark gray for the main text of your CV. Dark blue or medium blue can be used as accent colors such as titles and bullet points.

- Remember that your CV is not an art project. It's a business document that should convey your professionalism and expertise. Show personality, but always err on the side of professionalism.

- Are your margins ragged? Do you have too many hyphenated words that result in a messy look? Are there any drastic changes in font size that create a sense of imbalance?

- Don't be verbose. If you can make a point in a single sentence, do so. Attorneys are busy and want you to get to the point.

- Keep your CV under two pages. Focus on key points and career highlights. This is not an autobiography; clients can get to know you better after they've hired you.

If you're still unsure whether your CV is ready to send to potential clients, it might be worthwhile to hire a professional resume writer or editor to review the document and provide suggestions. They'll often find an improvement or two, but more importantly, the extra review will give you an extra bit of confidence as you pursue new business. To succeed as an LNC, you need all the well-earned confidence you can get.

YOUR LETTER OF INTRODUCTION

When you applied for your last nursing job, you likely included a cover letter that was customized to the position you sought. You'll be writing

~ 27 ~

similar letters as an LNC, although we now call this document a letter of introduction.

When you become a legal nurse consultant, you will no longer be responding to online job postings; instead, you'll be reaching out to attorneys that you believe can use your services. You'll often be contacting attorneys cold, with no personal introduction from a mutual acquaintance. This is where a strong letter of introduction comes in to play,

Your letter of introduction should be customized to each attorney you reach out to. Here are a few tips:

- Focus on each attorney's unique needs. Start and end your letter of introduction with specific statements about how you can help. What can you do for them that no one else can?

- Research each attorney to whom you write, and get to know their practice well enough to tailor your letter their areas of expertise.

- Make sure to include specific information about your background and experience that directly relates to the attorney's clients; demonstrate the ways that your expertise meets the attorney's specific needs.

- If possible (and if you have permission), mention other attorneys with whom you have worked with on similar cases and who will vouch for you.

- Indicate that you're available for a brief informational meeting, either in person or by phone, so you can chat more about how you can be of service and answer any questions they may have.

~ 28 ~

CRUSH IT: THE LEGAL NURSE BLUEPRINT FOR SUCCESS

As with your CV, ask a professional or a trusted friend to review your letter of introduction before sending it to a potential client. A small spelling error can put the kibosh on your other efforts, so this document must be perfect.

Once you're confident that both your CV and letter of introduction are as strong as they can possibly be, start sharing them! These are documents you will want to attach in any introductory emails to attorneys who may turn in to clients.

BRANDING BASICS

Starting a new business--even if you're its only employee—requires thinking about how your business will be perceived publicly and what makes it stand out.

You want to build your LNC brand intentionally and authentically. Think of the positive aspects of your personality and experiences that you want to convey to your potential clients. Your brand should attract your ideal clients, build trust, and help them get to know and like you.

Developing a solid brand from the get-go can help underscore the consistency that will eventually make you a memorable and recognizable LNC.

Generally, a brand consists of both written and visual elements that communicate feelings and ideas describing who you are and what you have to offer.

~ 29 ~

Expect to take some time to develop a brand you love, but don't let this step stop you from getting started as an LNC. Plenty of new business owners have no idea how they want to brand themselves. Heck, plenty of huge companies constantly rebrand and reposition themselves.

Branding will be an ongoing and important part of your business. As a new LNC, keep in mind that any logo or branding you share publicly will be noticed. Make deliberate, well-considered choices.

Consistency is vital when launching a new business. Ideally, your business name, website domain name and social media handles will all be the same, or at least very similar; this basic type of consistency helps build your brand while avoiding confusion.

Is your business name:

- Catchy and relevant?
- Easy to pronounce and spell?
- Unique enough not to be mistaken for a similar business?

Don't forget that your business name will follow you and grow with you wherever your LNC business takes you. Spend some time to decide on a name that feels right for you.

MAKING IT OFFICIAL: BUYING YOUR DOMAIN NAME

You may not be ready to build your website today, but one day soon you will, and you're going to need a domain name. Don't let this be an afterthought: it's an important part of your branding efforts, and changing domain names once your business is up and running can be tremendously costly.

CRUSH IT: THE LEGAL NURSE BLUEPRINT FOR SUCCESS

To purchase and register a domain name you must go through a registrar. If you're not ready to actually build your website, but want to use a custom domain name for professional emails, you might consider a registrar-only service like the one offered by GoDaddy.com. If you're ready to launch a professional website, your hosting company can register a domain name for you as part of your subscription.

Choosing an appropriate and unique domain name with a business-friendly .com extension may take some research. While purchasing the domain name itself is a relatively intuitive task, finding the right name may not be so simple, since many desirable URLs have already been claimed by other businesses. If you don't already own your name as a domain (firstname+lastname.com), try to purchase it right now. This is the first step toward protecting and maintaining your personal and professional online reputation. If you've named your business something other than your name, look for that next. Registering a few different domains isn't overkill: you can always redirect one URL to another later. Ideally, your domain name will match your business name, or be similar enough to your that people easily associate the two. For example, a business called "Super ABC" could have the domain name SuperABC.com or ABC.com. In any case, choose a domain name that's memorable and accessible. You may need to try several versions of your business name before you can make your purchase. Domain registrars will often suggest variations on names to aid you in your search. It's always best to choose .com as a top-level domain, but there are other options available: in a pinch, you might find that a domain name ending in .biz

~ 31 ~

or .net is preferable to the compromises you'll need to make to find a domain name ending in .com.

Here's a tip that I wish I knew when I was starting my own LNC business. If you're not set on a business name yet, consider searching for your domain name first. An available domain name that makes an impact may just be the best basis for your actual business name moving forward.

If you have your heart set on a specific business name and the ideal domain name has been registered by someone else, you can check to see if it is actually being used for an active website. If not, it may be available to purchase from the registered owner. Some domain registrars offer services to help broker these deals, but keep in mind that you will likely pay a premium: chances are good that the domain name you're after has been registered by speculators who will only release it for a considerable sum. Be open to variations of your preferred domain name to avoid falling prey to these domain-squatters.

Once you register your domain, creating a business email address is essential to making your business appear credible. After purchasing your domain name, you will have the option to set up an email account through your registrar. It may cost a little bit of money to do so, but it's a worthwhile expense. Imagine handing out business cards at a networking event with your domain name and a Gmail address as the best way to contact you! That would be a red flag to potential clients that you're an amateur in running a business. The goal here is to portray the utmost level of professionalism, and that portrayal will require some upfront expenditures.

YOUR VISUAL BRAND

Creating consistent visual elements is a critical part of building a memorable brand as an LNC. Once you have a logo designed, you can use it throughout your online and offline assets, such as in your social media accounts (see Chapter 4), your professional website (see Chapter 5), your email signature (see Chapter 7), and at events (see Chapter 9).

For example, my business is called National Nurse Consulting and my tagline is "Your Case. Your Success. Our Business". My logo incorporates each of these elements cleanly into a single identifiable brand.

We'll dive deeper into your online presence in the following chapters, but consider your social media profiles as key parts of your branding. Don't wait too long before reserving the names for your business-related social media accounts and using your logo to consistently start building brand awareness.

NATIONAL NURSE
— C O N S U L T I N G —

Ideally your business name, domain name, and social media profiles (Facebook, LinkedIn, Twitter, Instagram) should all be consistent. Grab your social media handles and domain name today before someone else does!

JANICE DOLNICK BSN, RN, LNC

Here's a quick worksheet to get you brainstorming about your brand.

Possible Business Names:

✓ _____

✓ _____

✓ _____

Possible Taglines:

✓ _____

✓ _____

✓ _____

Available Domain Names:

✓ _____

✓ _____

✓ _____

Available Social Media Accounts:

✓ _____

✓ _____

✓ _____

✓ _____

✓ _____

CRUSH IT: THE LEGAL NURSE BLUEPRINT FOR SUCCESS

Ideas for Visual Branding

✓ _____

✓ _____

✓ _____

✓ _____

✓ _____

CHAPTER FOUR
CRAFTING YOUR ONLINE PRESENCE

Social media marketing for LNCs

Social media marketing tends not to be a major priority for us nurses, nor a particular strength. Sure, we spend time browsing Facebook and sharing pictures with our family and friends. But there's seldom a good reason to craft a unique social media presence when you're working tough shifts at the hospital, even if there were enough hours in the day.

However, in case you haven't noticed, social media these days is used for more than posting cat videos and birthday greetings. It's also an amazing opportunity for entrepreneurs to use platforms like LinkedIn, Facebook, Instagram, and Twitter to brand themselves, reach potential clients, and turn those clients into repeat customers.

WHY LNC ENTREPRENEURS NEED A SOCIAL MEDIA STRATEGY

One of the first rules of business is to always be where your clients are.

While in-person networking is very important (see Chapter 9), the reality is that most of us are too busy to personally build a large and solid enough network to sustain our businesses. We're also all glued to our laptops and smartphones, for better or for worse. Social media is an amazing

~ 37 ~

opportunity to reach out to busy attorneys and start to build your profile and client base remotely.

Social media platforms can also drive traffic to your website (see Chapter 5) as you begin to grow your business and brand. If you're already feeling overwhelmed , please take a deep breath with me right now. Let's do this together, one step at a time.

You don't have to be active on every single platform, every single day, straight out of the gate when you launch your business. However, you do need to begin building your presence online in order to compete with the thousands of other LNCs using these tools to reach clients and secure business. Let's start by looking at the most important social media tools for entrepreneurs.

LinkedIn

If you're just getting started with social media for business and personal marketing, start here. LinkedIn is the most popular professional social networking site in the world; as of the writing of this book, I believe that LinkedIn is the most powerful social media platform for LNCs.

Not only does LinkedIn act as an online CV and showcase your experience and skill-set 24/7, it's also a way to build your network, find new business, and become a thought leader.

Your LinkedIn page (here's a link to mine or visit https://www.linkedin.com/in/nationalnurseconsulting/) should include the same information that you have in your CV, but communicated in a

CRUSH IT: THE LEGAL NURSE BLUEPRINT FOR SUCCESS

less formal manner. The ideal LinkedIn profile includes your headshot, business information, branding, professional summary, details about your employment background and education, a list of your unique skills, testimonials, and contact information.

Always keep in mind that everything you present on social media reflects the type of work product that you'll be providing to your attorney clients. Make sure that your LinkedIn profile is complete and presentable. Treat LinkedIn as if it's the only thing that an attorney will see before hiring you, because it just might be.

You can and should post and share content on LinkedIn that's relevant to your ideal client. For example, you might link to articles of interest to your network, or sit down and write a blog post about LNC issues. Sharing content is a proven way to remain atop the minds of potential clients, build credibility, and display thought leadership.

Be sure to log in to your LinkedIn profile at least once a week. Before long, you probably won't need any reminders to do so: LinkedIn is a great tool for researching and connecting with potential clients and learning more about their businesses, their personal interests, and even their pain points.

In this business, like so many others, it's not so much what you know, but who you know. What makes LinkedIn such an amazing resource is that you can showcase who you are as a professional legal nurse consultant while also easily connecting with others who are active on the platform.

~ 39 ~

LinkedIn is like a cocktail party where everyone you could ever want to meet is in attendance. First you will want to connect with the people you know in real life, just like most of us gravitate towards friends at the start of an event. Before long, you'll be comfortable enough to make new connections by simply sending an attorney a short message introducing yourself. I recommend using the following script to connect with strangers who may turn into potential clients down the road:

Hi [First Name]. Hope to connect. Have a great week! ~ [Your Name]

That's it! You don't have to think of something clever or even send them any kind of sales pitch. You wouldn't do that at an in-person networking event, and you shouldn't do that on LinkedIn either. You simply want to start growing your network and building relationships so that you can take business conversations *off* the platform and into the real world through an email, a phone call, or an in-person meeting.

Once someone connects with you on LinkedIn, they will be able to see your full profile and any content you share on the platform. This alone will keep you on their minds the next time they need an LNC. You can also move things forward by sending them a message and seeing if they might be open to starting a business conversation.

A script for that sort of suggestion might look something like this:

Hi [First Name].

Thank you for connecting so quickly. Let me know if you're ever interested in chatting more.

Warmest Regards,

[Your Name]

[Your Business Name] / [Your Business Tagline]

Again, you're not sending them a hard sales pitch or making demands of them. You're simply putting yourself on potential clients' radar and making yourself and your business known.

Most of us love meeting new people, especially those who may be able to help us with our own interests. Your goal with LinkedIn is to demonstrate your professional value and expand your professional network with those who may have the power to hire you one day.

FACEBOOK

As of February 2019, 2.23 billion people log in to Facebook every month, and 65% of those people use it daily. You read that right. Billions of people.

This means that you can reach many professionals on Facebook, including attorneys and other legal professionals. That is an opportunity that simply cannot be ignored.

Many attorneys get so caught up in their cases and trials that they don't reach out for help. I stay on their radar through a Facebook Business page [https://www.facebook.com/nationalnurseconsulting/] where I share content, and by running ads specifically aimed at attorneys. Maintaining an active presence on as many platforms as possible could mean that the next time an attorney requires assistance on their medical-related legal cases, you're the one they'll call!

~ 41 ~

Facebook also reminds previous clients that they can hire you again, and lets you connect with new attorneys in various legal specialties. It's another important step in raising your profile and building trust among your new professional community.

Once your Facebook Business page is set up, be sure to add your logo, tagline, location, and service offerings. This is part of creating a memorable experience for anyone visiting your business page, and building a recognizable brand.

Creating content for your Facebook Business page may seem difficult at first, but it's quite simple once you get started. Here are some ideas on what you can post about:

- How you, as a legal nurse entrepreneur, can assist attorneys in their work
- Important information that attorneys know but forget
- Important information that attorneys may not be aware of
- Other people's content that's relevant to attorneys (properly credited, of course)
- Information about an upcoming training event that you or a colleague will be hosting

If you're still stuck on what to write about, you can ask some trusted legal professionals in your network what they would like to know about and answer their questions before they even have to ask. Remember that any content you create for your Facebook Business page can also be used on LinkedIn, and vice versa.

CRUSH IT: THE LEGAL NURSE BLUEPRINT FOR SUCCESS

TWITTER

Twitter appeals to a slightly different audience than LinkedIn and Facebook, and has lost favor in some circles. But it's still a good channel for anyone looking to elevate their position as an industry thought leader. If you want to be plugged in to breaking news and connect with journalists who might be interested in interviewing you for a story they're working on about a case, Twitter is still the place to be.

A Twitter presence can help build your professional network, even if it doesn't provide much of a showcase for your skills and experience. If you're not interested in actively participating on Twitter, at least consider setting up a private account just for listening in, following others in the legal space, and watching for breaking news and trends that might impact your business. If you can spot a newsworthy item, you can share it with current or potential clients to keep your business on their minds.

Remember that you should add your Facebook, LinkedIn, and Twitter URLs to the following:

- Invoices
- Your CV
- Your letter of introduction
- Your business cards
- Your business marketing materials
- Your signature on professional emails
- Outgoing snail-mail business correspondence
- Comments that you leave on blogs by other professionals

~ 43 ~

- Any other social media accounts you may have

USING SOCIAL MEDIA TO BUILD COMMUNITY

The fun isn't over! LinkedIn, Facebook, and Twitter are amazing tools for building your business, and I know from experience that using them regularly will help you achieve your goals.

Being a legal nurse consultant isn't always easy, and it can get lonely at times. One of the other great advantages of actively using social media is connecting with others. Whenever you find yourself feeling stressed or overwhelmed, remember that you can always reach out to other trusted legal nurse consulting entrepreneurs via social media, and they will likely be able to sympathize.

Don't delay this important step. Get active on social media and start building your presence, and your business, today.

CHAPTER FIVE
CREATING THE PERFECT WEBSITE

First impressions matter

While social media can help you connect with others in your field, the heart of your online presence should be an asset that you fully own and control. Your business website is an absolute necessity as it will attract potential clients, explain what you can do for them, and collect their contact information.

WHY YOU NEED A WEBSITE

To put it simply, owning and developing a website is a must if you want to be taken seriously as a legal nurse consultant and as an entrepreneur.

While LinkedIn, Facebook, and Twitter are critical to developing your online presence, they are no substitutes for your own website. Think of your website as your home base and your first opportunity to make an impression on potential clients. It should encourage attorneys to get to know you, find out what you have to offer, and feel like they're working with a reputable, established professional.

A well-developed website allows your current and prospective clients to locate you quickly and gives your existing clients an easy way to refer their colleagues to you. A website can also act as a vehicle for collecting leads, sharing content, and providing samples of your work.

~ 45 ~

You'll have a wide range of options when setting up your business entity online. New products and services hit the market all the time, and today's best practices may not be tomorrow's. That said, you'll want to start with two basic steps:

1.   Register a domain name if you haven't already (see Chapter 3 for more on this).

2.   Select a host for your website.

Once you have chosen and purchased your domain name, you will need to find a company to "host" your website so that it can be published and available online for the world to see. You should be able to accomplish each of these steps through the same company: many domain registrars also offer in-house website hosting, and many web hosts have relationships with domain registrars that allow you to choose a domain and set up your web space in one transaction.

Of course, you can also register a domain using one service and buy hosting through an entirely different company. It all comes down to your budget and your comfort level with this more technical side of getting set up online. Different hosts charge different prices, typically on an annual basis. Popular web hosts as of this writing include GoDaddy, Bluehost, and SiteGround. Feel free to ask your fellow LNCs for hosting recommendations, or your web developer if you plan to use one.

USE A PROFESSIONAL EMAIL ADDRESS

As we discussed in Chapter 3, if you haven't already set up a professional email address, now is the time. This is a huge step toward establishing

CRUSH IT: THE LEGAL NURSE BLUEPRINT FOR SUCCESS

your professionalism as a legal nurse . It's hard to take an entrepreneur seriously if they are conducting business from a personal Gmail or Hotmail account.

For your email, you will want HIPPA-compliant formatting so that you can work with attorney clients who accept specific types of legal cases. HIPAA (Health Insurance Portability and Accountability Act of 1996) is United States legislation whose data-privacy and security provisions are designed to safeguard medical information. You cannot get this service through a free email service provider. Any established web host can provide you with appropriate encryption as well as the HIPPA-compliant formatting, but it's worth your time to confirm that you'll be getting what you need.

Encryption helps keep any information transmitted to you confidential and safe, whether that's information received directly from an attorney, or secondhand from their clients.

WEBSITE DEVELOPMENT: PROFESSIONAL DESIGN VS. DIY

Most of us legal nurse consultants have wide-ranging skill sets, but building and coding websites is not typically among them. To create a website, most of us are wise to hire a professional website developer to ensure that the result looks clean and professional, and that it works as intended. Some good DIY options are available that let you create your own web sites (e.g. Squarespace and Wix), but I highly recommend investing in a professional job.

~ 47 ~

Remember that you will be competing with thousands of other legal nurse consultants nationwide, all of whom provide services identical or similar to yours. Every single one of the most successful legal nurse consultants I know have invested in professionally designed websites. If you want to compete for big business, you need to put your best foot forward. If you'd hire a professional contractor to build a storefront business, you should consider taking the same approach to your online presence.

Untold thousands of web designers and developers are capable of building the sort of web site you'll need, and each charges differently for their services. As a new LNC, you will likely not have a huge budget for your website, and that's okay. Shop around and find someone at a price point that you're comfortable with.

Your needs, from a coder's perspective, are relatively simple and straightforward. Your new website doesn't need every bell and whistle available, so don't be suckered in to paying huge amounts of money. Make it clear to whomever you hire that you simply need a website that incorporates current best practices, showcases your brand, and looks clean and professional. You also want to be sure your new website can grow with you as your business expands and evolves.

ARE YOU A DIYER?

While I always recommend hiring a professional and staying away from the free website builders, I know that some folks are born DIYers who will insist on building their websites themselves. If you enjoy dabbling in this area and have some experience in website development, this may be just the project for you. For new LNCs with DIY ambitions but little coding

CRUSH IT: THE LEGAL NURSE BLUEPRINT FOR SUCCESS

experience, some affordable solutions are available that offer drag-and-drop-style website-building tools.

If you decide to build your website yourself, please remember that this is the first impression many clients will have of your business. Make sure that the result is something that you will be proud to share with your network, and that it serves as an effective calling card for new business as a legal nurse consultant.

SEARCH ENGINE OPTIMIZATION

Search engine optimization, or SEO, is the practice of writing and coding your website so that it pops to the top of search-result pages. You'll want to ensure your website developer (or you as a DIYer) is well-versed in the latest SEO developments. With solid SEO behind it, your website will be among the first listed by search engines like Google when potential clients search for legal nurse consulting services.

A high-quality website development team can provide SEO services to help you maximize your website's visibility. Some companies even offer SEO-optimized copywriting services. The bottom line is that you want your website content to be easily discoverable while remaining engaging, informative, and easy to read.

WHAT DO I PUT ON MY WEBSITE?

The next thing to consider is what pages and content need to be on your business website. Let's start by discussing your main page, otherwise known as your home page.

~ 49 ~

Throughout my years working with attorneys, I have learned that what potential clients really want to know is **what you can do for them**. They want this information as directly and quickly as possible. Your home page should fulfill this need while also showcasing who you are as an LNC.

Avoid cluttering up your home page with too much text. This can be overwhelming, and a disorderly website will reflect poorly on you as an LNC. Imagine it from an attorney's perspective: if your website is chaotic, what will working with you be like?

Above all, create a home page that conveys professionalism, intuitive navigation, and high-quality information. Then build the rest of your site around those same qualities.

LOGICAL WEBSITE ORGANIZATION

Visitors will land on your home page when they visit your URL, which matches the domain name you purchased. That first page should clearly explain what your business does and what you have to offer.

You will also likely create sub-pages that share more specific information, like your list of services, your areas of specialization, testimonials from clients, and contact information. Don't hesitate to add as many sub-pages as you need to tell your story. It's better to have a menu of well-organized pages than just one or two highly cluttered pages that try to do too much.

Common examples of sub-pages include:

- Home
- About

CRUSH IT: THE LEGAL NURSE BLUEPRINT FOR SUCCESS

- Services
- Testimonials
- Blog
- FAQs
- Contact

Try to keep your top-level menu clean and simple: not every page needs to be listed on your primary menu. For example, a page to schedule an appointment with you should probably be on a subpage of your "Contact us" menu item.

Here is a link [ntnlnurseconsulting.com] to my own company's website, which was designed by a professional. Feel free to use it as a guideline when brainstorming the kinds of pages you need for your own professional website.

WHAT CONTENT GOES WHERE?

Once you have decided which sub-pages to include on your website, you'll still need to organize your content and decide what goes where.

Here's a list to help you build your website in a logical manner. Feel free to add anything else that you believe is critical for your website's success:

Home:

- An introduction about you and what you have to offer as an LNC
- A call to action ("Contact me for a free consultation")

~ 51 ~

- Text and/or video explaining how you are different from other legal nurses
- Your areas of specialization
- Your phone number and e-mail address

About:

- Your professional biography and headshot
- A list of associations you're affiliated with

Services:

- A list of services you provide
- What types of cases you focus on
- What a client can expect when they work with you
- A call to action for a free consultation

Testimonials:

- Testimonials written by attorney clients

Blog:

- Your blog posts
- An e-newsletter subscription form

FAQs

- Questions and answers about legal nurse consulting
- Free resources or samples that showcase your work

Contact Us:

CRUSH IT: THE LEGAL NURSE BLUEPRINT FOR SUCCESS

- Your professional contact information
- Your office hours (if relevant)
- An easy-to-use contact form

Make sure that your website provides all the information a potential attorney client might require. A properly developed website will be a 24/7 marketing machine working on your behalf, and will become your virtual home base as a legal nurse consulting entrepreneur.

YOUR WEBSITE AND YOUR BRAND

Your website must be informative, but don't overlook the value of visual appeal and compelling branding. Design is important. Colors, fonts, and other elements combine to give visitors an overall impression not just of your website but of your entire business, and of you as a professional.

So what colors should you choose for your website? Work with your designer to develop an appropriate, on-brand color palette before getting started. The main color is important, but without the accent colors you won't know which colors to use for links, highlighted text, and other features.

Be consistent. Your website is an essential part of your overall branding, and it should be consistent with all the other elements of your business. Use the same color palette on your website and for your offline marketing materials like printed flyers and brochures. Reinforcing your brand online and offline helps people become acquainted and familiar with you and your business.

Select easy-to-read fonts and use them consistently. Even if you design and build your website yourself, advice from a professional graphic designer can go a long way to creating a look that reflects a professional image. This is all part of building a brand: a bit of initial investment can pay off quickly when it helps attract your first clients.

MAINTAINING YOUR WEBSITE

Regardless of how you choose to build your website, you need to plan how it will be maintained. Will you learn how to do this yourself, or will you hire someone to help you? Your website designer or developer may also offer a maintenance package and serve as your website administrator or webmaster. This is another question to ask before hiring someone to work on your website on your behalf.

A webmaster can be your long-term partner in keeping your website timely, secure, functional, and visible, even as the web-hosting landscape changes. A webmaster can also keep an eye on your analytics, which track your site's performance and identify opportunities to increase traffic. All of this encompasses the more technical side of being an entrepreneur, and is as important as the work you'll be contracted to perform as an LNC.

If you're not technically savvy and don't understand the inner workings of the internet, it's a good idea to develop a relationship with a professional web developer or webmaster and graphic designer to get your home base looking as professional as possible.

Just get started!

It's easy to get overwhelmed by all the decisions involved with creating your website. Don't let paralysis by analysis delay the opening of your

CRUSH IT: THE LEGAL NURSE BLUEPRINT FOR SUCCESS

business. This is a mistake I see time and time again, and it's a biggie. Nothing trumps experience as a legal nurse consultant, so get something online and get working!

From concept to launch and into the maintenance phase, consider your skills, interests and available time when you consider how to tackle creating your website. Reflect on your priorities when deciding on how to get started.

Remember that you can start with a simple, inexpensive website. This is just the beginning. Jumping in sooner rather than later will give you a better understanding of what you want to include on your website as your business grows. Most importantly, don't get bogged down with design decisions and technical concerns. Leave that to the professionals. Just get started…and don't forget to have fun with the process.

Chapter Six
Blogging Your Heart Out!

Be a content maven

TO BLOG OR NOT TO BLOG

Getting your website to the first page of Google's search results is a tall order and a worthy goal. It might not be your aim right now, but you can at least plan to get your site seen by more and more people, which will result in more and more business. The fastest and easiest way to accomplish this is through blogging.

Your website alone may not immediately bring you the clients that you want. However, including a blog on your website allows you to more easily build and manage a network of likeminded contacts and prospects. It also provides content to share on your social media platforms, which we discussed in Chapter 4 as an effective way to differentiate yourself in the crowded LNC market.

This is especially true once you have established yourself as a professional who is both an expert in the medical field and a trusted authority within the legal community. A well-written blog that includes the right LNC topics will demonstrate your expertise while persuading others to trust you and your professional opinion.

~ 57 ~

THE MORE YOU BLOG, THE HIGHER YOU RANK

Without due attention to SEO, your website will likely only be seen by those you directly ask to visit it. Your goal is to draw traffic while you sleep, attracting a stream of prospects to add to your marketing funnel. No matter how carefully planned or engagingly designed your website may be, your online presence needs the right marketing tools behind it.

Fortunately, you can include keywords in the text of your website and on your blog that will draw the right kind of traffic to you, and with it the right kinds of prospective clients. The more targeted your keywords are, the more ideal your site visitors will be after finding your page through a search engine, and the likelier those visitors will be to become clients.

Your search engine ranking will improve with each relevant blog post you publish. It's that simple.

Like it or not, most material published on the Web requires a relatively short attention span, and readers have adjusted their habits accordingly. Your blog should follow suit. Remember to add images to make your blog more visually appealing and less overwhelmingly text-heavy. Also consider posting items that feature lists, or that make their cases in a series of brief points.

Also consider creating fact sheets and downloadable templates or tools and sharing them on your blog. Resources like these encourage repeat readership, which is exactly what you're after. You'll get your page bookmarked and likely get your services booked as well.

Remember that plenty of attorneys are waiting to receive the information you have at hand and the expertise you have to share. Put it out in the

CRUSH IT: THE LEGAL NURSE BLUEPRINT FOR SUCCESS

world and see what happens. Just make sure that it's engaging, relevant, and enjoyable to read.

TYING IT TOGETHER: YOUR BLOG AND SOCIAL MEDIA

Your attorney clients will get to know you through your blog, so be sure to post about a variety of topics that matter to them. What you write is important. You're the expert in your field, and attorneys may be looking for your medical knowledge when preparing for an arbitration or a trial. Be sure to mention your services occasionally throughout your blog, along with the reasons attorneys should hire you. Your website is yours, and you should use it to promote yourself while also providing valuable content. When your content speaks to what your potential clients want and need, they won't be able to get enough of it. Regularly posting new content to your blog gives attorneys a reason to keep coming back. It builds trust and makes them want to contact you for more specific advice and information. Don't forget to tie your blog posts back into your social media accounts. Share your posts on LinkedIn, Facebook and Twitter. This is how your content will spread and get seen by the right people. Others may even share your content with their own networks, multiplying its impact. You never know who might come across your blog and see your value as a consultant.

Along with consistently publishing solid content to your blog, you can improve your site's ranking in search engine results by including keywords in your posts that mirror the terms entered by searchers themselves. While

~ 59 ~

you always want to sound like yourself and not a robot, using keywords in your blog posts will get the right people reading what you have to say.

How do you choose the best keywords? First, do some research. Find out which words are most commonly used by prospective clients who are looking to hire LNCs. Many online resources are available to help identify the best keywords for your niche, including the <u>Google Keywords Tool</u> and <u>Keywoordtool.io</u>. Write down the most relevant and popular keywords in your niche and remember to use them in future blog posts. Many experienced bloggers begin with keyword research and use a list of keywords to guide their writing. Beginning with a list of keywords will help drive traffic to your website and help you decide what to write about.

WHY YOU'LL FALL IN LOVE WITH BLOGGING

Blogging is good for business, but it's also fun. Blogging offers you the opportunity to share what matters to you, your writing skills will inevitably improve, you'll raise your professional profile, and people will get to see what type of person you are and what you have to offer as an LNC in a way that a CV can't convey. Blogging can also be very social, particularly when you keep the tone of your blog light and friendly and leave the comments section on so that people can interact with your posts. Everyone who visits your blog should leave knowing a bit about you and encouraged to contact you. Website and blog visitors who don't book your services right away can still become important contacts who refer you to new clients. Those who do hire you will appreciate having been able to get to know you online before trusting you with valuable cases. As long as

CRUSH IT: THE LEGAL NURSE BLUEPRINT FOR SUCCESS

you carve out a bit of time each week to keep your content fresh, there's no downside to consistent blogging.

BUILD A COMMUNITY OF LIKE-MINDED PROFESSIONALS AND POTENTIAL CLIENTS

Everyone has a handful of favorite websites that always seem to be full of useful resources. So why not create your own? By simply adding social media buttons to your website and blog, you can create a space for a community of potential clients to hang out. You'll have the opportunity to network with them and watch your social following expand.

How do you do this? Ask questions in your posts that compel readers to engage and share. Allow a section for comments after each blog post, and get ready to meet your public.

All you need to do to become a blogger is to share as much useful information about your areas of expertise as you can. I recommend publishing a new blog post at least every week or two. Do this consistently and you'll see your sphere of influence grow; your business will follow suit. There are so many benefits of blogging: sharing your expertise, increasing your website traffic, building trust with prospective clients, attracting new business, even blowing off steam once in a while. We're lucky to have this opportunity to showcase our expertise, so don't let that opportunity pass you by!

CHAPTER SEVEN

EMAIL MARKETING

Creating familiarity with potential clients

While the digital landscape is constantly evolving, email marketing remains one of the most effective ways to keep your current clients engaged, reach new clients, and build your brand.

New channels of communication are being introduced so quickly these days that it's easy to be lured into thinking you must master every new online marketing fad that comes along. That's not a good use of your time, and it will only dilute your marketing efforts in the long run. If you're looking for a proven way to drive measurable results, make sure you have a strong email marketing strategy in place before you tackle other channels.

According to the Direct Marketing Association, email marketing on average delivers a 4,300% return on investment (ROI) for businesses in the United States. Yet small business owners often assume that email marketing isn't effective, or that it's too hard to develop and maintain a winning strategy.

Many people assume you need hundreds of people on an email list to justify the effort. That's not the case. Email marketing is frequently cited as the most cost-effective form of online marketing for small businesses

~ 63 ~

who do it right. These days, you can even automate and customize most of the process.

If you're new to email marketing, it may seem a bit daunting and complicated at first. Like anything else, it gets easier the more you do it. So jump in head first. You can do this, and you can start today.

A successful email strategy involves the following steps:

1. Build your email list and select your tools
2. Draft an email plan about what types of emails you will send
3. Design your email and create content
4. Automate, test and distribute your campaign
5. Analyze the results and tweak accordingly
6. Rinse and repeat!

Let's take a closer look at what you'll need to get started.

BUILD YOUR EMAIL LIST AND SELECT YOUR TOOLS

Before you think about sending your first marketing email, you'll want to choose a system to collect and manage your email addresses, create and segment lists, and collect data so that you can adjust future emails as necessary.

With so many email marketing tools out there, you may feel overwhelmed at first. It's important to bear in mind that you can get started with any of them, and that you'll be able to make wiser decisions only after you've gained some experience. It's also important to remember that you can always move your list and email marketing campaigns somewhere else

CRUSH IT: THE LEGAL NURSE BLUEPRINT FOR SUCCESS

later on if you feel like you have identified a better option. Nothing is ever set in stone.

I recommend starting with an email marketing tool that offers a free or low-cost trial, so you can get your feet wet without a huge investment.

New tools become available constantly, but as of this writing here are some of the more popular options:

- Mailchimp
- Constant Contact
- Active Campaign
- AWeber

Mailchimp offers a completely free service up to a certain number of subscribers, but with limited customer support unless you upgrade to one of their paid plans. Constant Contact offers a free 30-day trial and is a popular choice for small businesses. You must pay for AWeber, but it's relatively affordable and very well-rounded.

Take a little bit of time to do some research and then just pick one and get started. Don't waste too much time and effort agonizing over the right decision before you get in there and develop a better idea of what works best for you.

If you're completely new to email marketing, you may want to check out a book that is specifically about that topic. Browse Amazon's bestsellers on the subject or visit your local library and just pick one to read. You don't need to become the most advanced email marketing expert ever; you

~ 65 ~

just need an idea about how to set appropriate goals and how to achieve them. You can also check out the free tutorials offered by most email marketing providers. They want you to become a long-term customer, so most services offer videos with clear instructions that walk you through the steps of setting up your first campaign.

CONSIDER ADDING A LEAD CAPTURE FORM TO YOUR WEBSITE

While not mandatory, a simple signup form on your website that allows visitors to learn more about you and your services will help you build your list more quickly.

Consider adding an opt-in or lead-capture form in several places on your website, directing people to sign up to learn more about you, or to subscribe to your e-newsletter. This is something that your web designer can help you with.

Be sure to include text explaining what visitors are signing up for when they provide their email address. Include a form on your Contact page, but also on any landing page where you have an offer, and possibly on your home page as well.

If you have any plans for operating in Canada or in the European Union, make sure you and your webmaster comply with the GDPR (General Data Protection Regulation) guidelines. This regulation took effect May 18, 2018. Its purpose is to:

- support privacy as a fundamental human right

CRUSH IT: THE LEGAL NURSE BLUEPRINT FOR SUCCESS

- require businesses that handle personal data to be accountable for managing that data appropriately
- give individuals rights over how their personal data is processed or used

Your email service provider should offer clear guidelines to help you comply with the GDPR, You can find the complete GDPR regulations at https://ec.europa.eu/info/law/law-topic/data-protection_en.

BUILDING YOUR EMAIL LIST

A quick way to start building your email list is to add email addresses that you have collected through your own personal networks, from previous clients, via professional associations, at networking events, and on social media. You must also legally always offer an easy way for your contacts to opt out of commercial communications if they do not want to continue receiving emails from you.

Continue building your list even when you think you have a big enough audience and plenty of leads. Collecting these addresses and leads for your business is not a one-time activity: it's an ongoing effort that will help you grow your business for years to come.

WHAT'S YOUR PLAN?

Now that you've set your email collection machine in motion, it's time to decide what types of emails you will send.

Sending a monthly email newsletter is a good place to start if you have the discipline, time, and resources necessary to ensure that you publish consistently. You want to deliver real value to your clients and potential clients through these emails, rather than sending purely promotional messages. Mix in promotional messages with educational messages and even a bit of just fun stuff.

Consider including the following:

- Case studies
- General business announcements
- Interview with an attorney client
- Industry news
- Reviews of recently published educational works
- A summary of your latest blog post, linked to the post itself
- Notifications of educational or networking events
- Something fun and light but still relevant to your business
- Seasonal messages for holidays and special events

MAKE YOUR EMAIL MARKETING APPEALING

Now it's time for the fun part! Almost all email marketing tools offer pre-designed templates to make sending attractive emails easy. You can use one of these templates or have one designed just for you. Don't overthink this part. As your business grows, you may want to invest in a full branding package whose email template matches your other marketing materials. When you're just getting started, it's more important to just get out there and get marketing.

CRUSH IT: THE LEGAL NURSE BLUEPRINT FOR SUCCESS

Make sure that your design is mobile-responsive. As with your website, you want to make sure that emails appear appropriately on whatever device your reader is using. Ready-made templates from any major email marketing tool should have this functionality built in.

Be sure to keep your emails brief, professional, personalized, and goal-oriented. The key is to properly research the contacts on your email list before sending anything out so that the emails you send will grab their attention, make an impact, and remain in their inbox (and on their minds).

SEGMENTING CONTACTS AND CUSTOMIZING CONTENT

At first, you will likely be sending emails to a single set of contacts. As your list grows, however, you can start thinking about how you will categorize your contacts according to their interests, a process called segmentation. You can even create multiple contact lists to make sure you're sending the right marketing messages to the right audiences.

You may want to consider segmenting based on:

- Practice specialty (e.g. personal injury, criminal, malpractice)
- Geographic location
- Your current clients
- Your prospective clients
- Email engagement (subscribers who open all your emails vs. those who don't)

~ 69 ~

- Personal relationship with you

INCLUDE A CALL TO ACTION

Your emails should always include a call to action (CTA). A CTA tells readers what you want them to do after reading your message, and should include a button that sends readers to your website or social media account. Think about the actions you want your reader to take that are beneficial to your business. For example, you might want to ask readers to:

- Read an article on your blog
- Contact you for a free consultation
- Connect with you on LinkedIn, Facebook or Twitter
- Download a case study or free resource

GRAB THEIR ATTENTION

Take some time to consider each email's subject line. We all get hundreds of emails a day, and we ignore or discard many of them based on their subject lines. Think about what subject lines and content make *you* decide to open an email. Approach your email marketing with that same voice. Just like you, your contacts don't want to be sold to; they want to *connect*.

AUTOMATE, TEST AND SEND YOUR EMAIL

Before you send your email to your list of contacts, be sure to test it by sending it to yourself, and if possible to a trusted friend or business associate as well. You want to make sure that it renders well on a variety

CRUSH IT: THE LEGAL NURSE BLUEPRINT FOR SUCCESS

of devices (desktop computer, tablet, smart phone), has no spelling or grammatical errors, and is engaging.

It's always a good idea to have a second set of eyes on your email content to catch little quirks and errors. Remember, you're positioning yourself as a thought leader, and typos or boring content can derail that effort.

Once you have reviewed your email and made any necessary revisions, it's time to send it to your list. This can be a little nerve-wracking at first (it was for me!), but just hit Send and see what kind of response it receives.

Always include yourself in the contact list so you can see when and how the email actually appears in an inbox. No matter how diligently you test and review your emails prior to sending, there may be an occasional glitch or item you missed, and it's always best if you're the first person to spot the mistake so you can note it for next time or send a revised and corrected version of the email.

ANALYZE THE RESULTS AND TWEAK ACCORDINGLY

Email marketing services provide you with the opportunity to analyze the performance of each message you send through a function called analytics. By getting familiar with your email service's user dashboard and its analytics capabilities, you'll be able to assess many key performance indicators (KPI) and determine how you might improve the results of your email campaigns.

Important KPIs to follow include:

- Open Rate: how many subscribers opened your email

~ 71 ~

- Click-Through Rate: how many subscribers followed a link in your email
- Conversion: how many subscribers completed a desired action
- Unsubscribe: how many subscribers opted out of your list after receiving your email
- Delivery: how many emails were successfully delivered
- Spam reports: how many subscribers reported your email as spam

Any good email marketing tool will share these analytics with you every time you send something out to your list. If you notice that certain types of emails are not being opened, or are not performing as well as others, you can look for ways to improve future campaigns.

RINSE & REPEAT!

Once you have the process down and feel confident that you're providing your email subscribers with useful content that they want to receive, it's time to schedule regular email campaigns to stay in touch and remain top of mind, as professional marketers put it. You don't want to inundate your audience with too many emails, but you also don't want them to forget that they subscribed to your list.

Keeping subscribers regularly engaged with content of real value increases the likeliness that they will open your emails and respond to your calls to action.

Once you've gotten a handle on the email marketing cycle, you can automate large parts of the process. As long as you write compelling

CRUSH IT: THE LEGAL NURSE BLUEPRINT FOR SUCCESS

content, the business of crafting emails and sending them to appropriate contacts can be largely handled automatically.

For example, you can create an automated campaign with emails that are sent when an individual subscriber meets a predefined trigger, such as subscribing to your list from an opt-in form on your website. Your system can automatically send them a welcome email, then follow up a week later with an email containing links to your most popular blog posts. The following week, maybe you'll reach out to them to talk a bit about your services and your roster of happy clients. All without you having to do a thing. That's the time-saving genius behind email marketing automation.

CHAPTER EIGHT
THE POWER OF THOUGHT LEADERSHIP

Author your own destiny

Once you get the hang of social media, blogging, and email marketing, you'll start to realize that you have a unique voice, an impressive library of content to draw from, and an extremely valuable LNC skill set.

Have you ever considered writing a book about your area of expertise? Publishing a book through a traditional publisher is no longer the only way to distribute your work to a worldwide audience. The ascendance of amazon.com and the emergence of other self-publishing platforms mean that anyone can share their expertise with the world.

Writing a book about your specific area of expertise marks you as an LNC thought leader. The very process of writing a book will also help you become a better communicator in general, which will help you advance as an LNC. It will also create an asset that you can sell, offering you the possibility of a passive income stream.

If writing and publishing a book sounds too daunting, keep in mind that times have changed. Getting a book published used to be a long shot; now it's something that anyone can do.

EBOOK VS. PAPER

If you're not ready to consider publishing a traditional bound book, consider starting with an ebook. You can even start by writing a very brief eBook that you make freely available for downloading on your website. Even a two- or three-page eBook can showcase your expertise and give you an edge on the competition. It will also help you grow your list of followers and act as a teaser to encourage potential clients to connect with you. eBooks also offer you the opportunity to include live links that send attorneys right back to your website.

Consider your book as another marketing tool. If you do decide to write a full-length book, it's best to have both electronic and print versions available: some of your audience will prefer reading on their devices, while others prefer the experience of holding a printed book in their hands. And some readers will be happy to buy both! Traditional publishers have tended to require the release of the printed book first, followed by an electronic version. This is no longer the only way to go, so do what works best for you.

BENEFITS OF AN EBOOK:

- Faster and less expensive to publish
- Faster and easier to share with others
- Immediate download caters to our need for instant gratification
- Busy attorneys are more likely to check out an electronic version on their devices while waiting for a meeting or during breaks from the courtroom

CRUSH IT: THE LEGAL NURSE BLUEPRINT FOR SUCCESS

- Links from your ebook can take your readers directly to additional information

BENEFITS OF A HARD COPY BOOK:

- Visibility: a printed book on a shelf or the desk will keep you top-of-mind
- You can use a print book like a physical calling card, much like a business card
- Underscores your authority when displayed at conferences and other events
- No need to charge up a device to read
- Some people prefer the tactile experience of holding a book
- For some audiences, a printed book carries more credibility than an ebook

GETTING STARTED

Focus on a very specific niche: the more specific, the better.

A detailed outline will be your best friend. Prepare an outline with the major subjects you plan to cover forming the chapters of your book, then create a detailed list of points under each chapter heading. Set a schedule for yourself and try to commit to drafting a pre-determined portion of your book each week, no matter what. If you already have a blog, you can even re-purpose some of that content as the basis of your book.

Don't get discouraged before you start. Your book doesn't have to be long. It doesn't have to win a Pulitzer Prize. It just has to convey value to readers and offer a unique point of view.

PREPARING TO PUBLISH: INVEST IN EDITING

Even if you were an English major or an award-winning journalist in a previous career, you need the services of an objective editor if you plan on publishing something beyond a few pages of work.

Even the best writers can be terrible editors of their own work. They know what they want to say, after all, and are naturally ready to make sense even of confusing passages, or to forgive grammatical quirks. A fresh set of eyes can more easily uncover basic typos and grammatical errors, along with broader issues of clarity, flow, and unity.

Lack of clarity is a common problem amongst books written by LNCs. Unclear references, ambiguous phrasing, and other errors of imprecision can confuse your readers. These types of errors may be particularly difficult for you to spot.

A good editor will also review your work for coherence and flow, which means moving from one idea to the next gracefully and logically. You don't want to lose your readers by skipping around and leaving them frustrated.

It can be hard to share your manuscript with someone else. It can be tempting to rush it to publication. And it can cost a bit of money to hire

CRUSH IT: THE LEGAL NURSE BLUEPRINT FOR SUCCESS

a professional editor. One way or another, though, your manuscript simply isn't finished until someone else has gone over it thoroughly.

SELECT A SERVICE FOR DESIGN AND PUBLISHING

Whether you decide to publish your book as a paper volume or a digital edition, you need a great cover design and consistent, easy-to-read formatting. Some self-publishing companies offer design and formatting as part of their basic suite of services; some charge extra; some may not offer these services at all, and instead refer you to third-party designers.

Many options exist for publishing digital and hard-copy books. While I'm not recommending one service over another, here are few to check out:

- Amazon.com
- Standout Books
- Lulu
- BookBaby

Once you are a published author, whole new worlds open up to you. When your book is finally available, I'd love to hear about it. Until then, get writing!

Chapter Nine
Networking in the Real World

Be you and be memorable

Conferences and other professional events are perfect opportunities to market yourself and your business. While you can get your new business up and running by following the advice found in this book and building a solid online presence, nothing replaces face-to-face interaction.

Do a little research to identify professional events in your area that you can attend either as a general conferencegoer or as an exhibitor. Join a bar association or business council to find out what's going on locally. Join bar associations in other states to help grow your network outside of your immediate area. Subscribe to legal magazines and keep a keen eye out for conferences. Bar associations and conference sponsors often have newsletters that you can join to stay informed of upcoming events.

PREPARATION IS EVERYTHING

Register for events early, and learn as much as you can about their organizers, speakers, and even their attendees. Most conferences publish lists of participants well in advance; use these to learn a bit about each speaker, so that you're prepared for a conversation when you meet them.

~ 81 ~

You don't need to dig too deeply here: it's easy these days to learn things about a stranger that don't quite fit into polite conversation. However, it never hurts to know about the general interests of key conference attendees; this will help you prepare an elevator pitch and decide how you will position yourself and your business when you finally meet.

Before you go, write down your goals for the event. These goals can be as simple as "meet three new people" or as elaborate as "secure a meeting with a decision-making attorney". Don't put too much pressure on yourself, but do keep your goals and accomplishments in mind as motivation to stay focused and to represent your business proudly and well.

Be sure to bring business cards, and mingle during breaks in the action. Along with attorneys, seek out paralegals and legal secretaries who may be tasked with locating appropriate resources for the attorneys they support. You never know who might be able to help you land your next client.

WHAT DO I SAY?

Instead of starting up a conversation with your sales pitch, try starting with a question instead. Ask about an attorney's specialty, how long they've been practicing, or where they practice. Ask if the attorney has ever used the services of a legal nurse consultant. If it feels right, you can then discuss how you help attorneys, stressing the benefits of working with you. Preparing an elevator pitch that you can customize according to your audience will help you feel confident and comfortable.

CRAFT YOUR ELEVATOR PITCH

An elevator pitch is a brief persuasive statement of no more than 20 seconds that you can use to break the ice with new contacts and build connections. Your elevator pitch should also include your unique selling proposition, or USP : what makes you especially capable of delivering exactly what each client needs. Consider the following steps when crafting your elevator pitch:

- Introduce yourself
- Explain what you do
- Communicate your USP
- Engage with a question
- Practice

It's as simple as that. For many people, networking feels awkward or even scary at first, and that's okay. Everyone is nervous! Just remember that networking is like a muscle: the more you use it, the stronger it will become.

If you find yourself struggling during your first couple of events as an entrepreneur, that's okay. Try making it more fun for yourself by turning it into a little game. Give yourself 30 minutes to share your elevator pitch with three new contacts. If you accomplish your goal, give yourself a small reward.

Another idea is practicing your elevator pitch ahead of time with trusted family members and friends. They can give you feedback, and you will get a sense of what works and what sounds clunky.

At the end of the day, networking is all about meeting new people, having fun, and providing value. As the old saying goes, "people will forget what you said, people will forget what you did, but people will never forget how you made them feel". Make everyone you meet feel special and heard, and watch your business grow in return.

WORK THAT BOOTH!

Some events may give you the opportunity to purchase a booth or a table to showcase your business and hand out information. Many conferences include dedicated spaces where exhibitors and vendors gather to meet attendees.

Think of your audience when you're presenting your services at an event:

- Who will be attending and visiting your booth?
- What kind of information do they want?
- How can you deliver information to them in a way that's unique and appealing?
- How can you make yourself stand out?

Find creative ways to stand out and bring more people to your booth. Everyone likes a freebie, even attorneys. Order some giveaway items printed with your company's name, logo, and URL; attorneys seem to love coffee mugs and tumblers. Items like these will most likely be used regularly, and will help keep your name top-of-mind. Attach a business card to your giveaways so your prospects can add your name to their list of resources.

BE PREPARED

Invest in a professional sign and/or a tablecloth printed with your business name. Some events will include a sign as part of your registration, but some will not, so always bring your own marketing materials and be prepared to showcase your brand.

Here are other items you may want to consider for your comfort and convenience:

- A lightweight folding chair
- Drinking water and a healthy snack
- Breath mints
- Pads of paper and pens
- Chargers for your mobile phone and other devices

It's important to prepare in advance so you don't find yourself scrambling on the day of the event. You want attorneys to see you as poised, efficient, and confident; appearing harried and rushed might just ruin a valuable opportunity to promote your business.

BE FRIENDLY AND APPROACHABLE

Don't stand behind your booth quietly waiting for people to come up to you. Stand in front or slightly to the side of your booth and smile. Greet everyone who walks by your booth without launching into a sales pitch. Just be human and say hello!

Don't be discouraged if attorneys don't take the time to stop and learn about your services. They're probably just rushing off to the next session or to check in with the office. When possible, hand them a business card and flash a warm smile. That can be enough to prompt them to seek you out when they have a few minutes to spare. Be confident and don't be afraid to shine.

Get to know the other exhibitors. Other vendors work with attorneys, too, after all, and can be your referral partners. If they're aware of your services, they might just mention your name to their attorney clients who need your help. Just by striking up a conversation with a few of my fellow exhibitors, I've personally received referrals from insurance companies, bail bond services, and many others.

See if you can make friends with the event organizers as well. Offer to help set up or clean up. Sometimes they'll even extend a discount to those who pitch in. This also may lead to speaking opportunities for you down the road.

THE MAGIC OF BAR ASSOCIATION EVENTS

One of the very best ways to secure new clients is by developing non-work relationships with them first. Attorneys do business with people they know, like, and trust. One of my favorite and most effective ways for building my successful LNC practice has been through local bar association events.

Take the following steps to get out there and get recognized as a leader and as the go-to expert at your local bar association:

CRUSH IT: THE LEGAL NURSE BLUEPRINT FOR SUCCESS

Locate three local bar associations. Review their websites and look for the main contact person or administrator and a calendar of events.

- Call or email the main contact, introduce yourself, and inquire about the cost of becoming a member (yes, you can actually become a member).

- Ask about the cost of attending events as a non-member. If events aren't published on the association's website, ask for an events calendar as well.

- Show up! Be sure to bring your business cards with you, dress professionally, come with a smile, and be yourself. Attorneys are people too. Every month, plug into local bar association meetings to begin to build your network of attorneys. If you do this consistently, you'll see your business begin to flourish.

PROMOTE YOUR ATTENDANCE

Use your website, social media and email marketing list to promote your presence at every event you attend. Be sure to check in on Facebook, post a couple of photos on LinkedIn, and share a great takeaway on Twitter. Announce that you're an exhibitor at the event and that you'll be available to answer questions about legal nurse consulting. This is a great way to connect with fellow attendees and increase traffic to your booth.

OFFER YOUR SERVICES AS A SPEAKER OR PANELIST

Other than writing and publishing your own blog posts, content, and book, few things position you as a thought-leader quite as well as speaking at conferences and other professional gatherings.

Identify the event coordinators of conferences geared to the legal profession by scouring LinkedIn or by visiting their websites. Reach out to event coordinators as soon as possible to inquire about speaking opportunities. Event coordinators are eager to feature new topics and speakers, so don't be shy about putting yourself forward.

Prepare a pitch letter or letter of introduction to send as a proposal. This doesn't have to take a lot of time. Simply write down several topics that you feel you have the expertise to cover, and add copy points for each. Include a few summaries of stories or case studies illustrating each major point you're addressing. Make it interesting and engaging.

Once you get a nibble on your offer, work with the event coordinator to customize your presentation to appeal to the specific audience they're trying to please. This isn't an imposition: they will be grateful that you took the time to ask.

Once you're clear on your target audience, complete your presentation and practice until you have it down cold. Prepare answers for any obvious questions that may arise, and have a list of resources to share with the audience members seeking more information (including your website, of course).

CRUSH IT: THE LEGAL NURSE BLUEPRINT FOR SUCCESS

After you deliver your presentation, take note of any questions or comments from your audience. This can give you great material for enhancements of future presentations and is a great source of topics to blog about.

While it may be nerve-wracking at first, becoming a go-to speaker about the legal nurse consulting industry can become an important asset in your marketing arsenal. Once you have one presentation down, you should be able to customize it quickly and easily for a variety of audiences.

CHAPTER TEN
NEVER STOP PROSPECTING

Keep your funnel full and create an endless referral cycle

We have certainly covered a lot of information in this book. Start today on putting together all the pieces we've discussed and working on the tactics you've learned, and you'll be well on your way to scrapping your scrubs forever.

Becoming a legal nurse consultant is the most fun and rewarding decision I have ever made. Since launching my business, I've never looked back at an emergency room, and have even started a beautiful family that I get to watch grow by choosing my own hours and working from home. Now it's your turn to take the leap!

Start brainstorming business names, secure your domain, and get your website ready. Get out there with social media, email marketing, blogging, thought leadership, public speaking, networking, cold calling…whatever it takes.

Remember that these tools are not discrete. They all feed into each other to strengthen your business and are most powerful when they're used in concert.

USE THE RESOURCES AT YOUR DISPOSAL

Meet a trusted friend for coffee and tell them that you're thinking of becoming a legal nurse consulting entrepreneur. Speaking aloud about your dreams can be your first major step toward turning those dreams into reality. Take at least one baby step each day toward establishing your business. Start to ask your former and current coworkers and clients for referrals and testimonials. These small but important steps can get the ball rolling and give you the confidence you need to dive head-first into your new venture.

At the end of the day, legal nurse consulting is all about credibility and referrals. I can't tell you how many referrals I've received simply by asking a couple of attorneys in my network to write a testimonial on my behalf. Every time I complete a case, I ask for a short statement about my services that I can post on my website. Never has an attorney said "no" to that request. Typically, attorneys are excited to write recommendations.

Remember the rule of reciprocity. Can you write a recommendation for someone in your network with whom you've worked closely? Could some of these contacts write one for you as well? It's human nature to reciprocate kindness. Maybe you were particularly impressed with how an attorney handled a case, how he treated his clients, how his staff worked as a team...these types of observations are all potential aspects of a recommendation that you can post on LinkedIn.

If you're just getting started and are struggling to get those first few testimonials, consider taking on some pro bono or volunteer work to grow

CRUSH IT: THE LEGAL NURSE BLUEPRINT FOR SUCCESS

your network and bring in recommendations. Get yourself out there, make some clients happy, and collect those testimonials.

MAKE YOUR CLIENTS FEEL SPECIAL.

Keep the contact information of all your clients and contacts in a customer relationship management (CRM) program or even just a spreadsheet. A well-organized list will let you sort your contacts in several valuable ways later on. Include clients' names, addresses, phone numbers, office hours, assistants' names, spouses' names, and even their birth dates. The best thing about knowing someone's birthday is that you can send them something small but special.

It may sound corny, but I can't tell you how many attorneys have brought me new business because I make them feel special and seen. I even get text messages with pictures of the gifts on their desks. This makes me smile since I know I helped to brighten their day.

As nurses, it's in our nature to make people feel better and I love that we can incorporate that into our business as legal nurse consultants. Make your clients feel special. They'll remember and take care of you when you do.

JOIN OUR COMMUNITY – WE CAN'T WAIT TO MEET YOU!

The community we've built at NNC-Members.com is a strong and supportive network where you can find professional resources and share client referrals. Connecting with your fellow LNCs can bring you a

~ 93 ~

considerable amount of work. When I get a lead for a case that falls outside my specialty, or my schedule is too full to accept a new case, I regularly subcontract work to NNC members. Many other LNCs do the same.

KEEP EXPANDING YOUR NETWORK

There is no excuse not to consistently generate new leads and referrals when we have all the resources we need at our fingertips.

It's as simple as using your favorite search engine to find attorneys who practice the type of law you specialize in. Hopping on social media, especially LinkedIn, connects you with attorneys in your area, which helps you keep adding potential clients to your list of prospects.

Of course, having a long list of leads won't do anything for you unless you reach out to them. Contact them by email or phone and ask for an appointment to meet and discuss your services. Use the elevator pitch you crafted in Chapter 9 to grab their attention. Send your perfect resume and letter of introduction. The key is to just keep working hard and making connections.

Develop your own procedure to systematically find and contact prospects and track their responses and your follow-up. This could be in a simple spreadsheet in Microsoft Outlook, a database program such as Access, or a more sophisticated CRM tool like Salesforce.

Keeping some type of record of your prospecting and outreach efforts will help you focus on next steps. Keep it simple at first and don't get

overwhelmed with learning new software. Stick with what you know when you're just starting out, and just get busy growing your business.

IT'S ALL IN THE FOLLOW-UP

Here's the reality: most attorneys you reach out to won't need your services immediately.

However, with the proper introduction and continued follow-up, you can make sure you remain top-of-mind when they or their colleagues *do* need your services.

Collect business cards from those you meet, and connect with them on social media. Send a personal note stating that you enjoyed meeting them, thanking them for their time, and offering to meet with them or schedule a call if they have any questions about how you might be able to assist them.

Building your relationships with attorney prospects through LinkedIn and other social media and email is great. But don't stop there. A traditional handwritten note will differentiate you from the competition and help you stand out. A piece of mail may also be seen and remembered by the attorney's administrative or paralegal support team, who can become valuable allies in your effort to gain new clients.

If an attorney you are speaking with doesn't have a need for your services right now, they may know someone who does. Attorneys know other attorneys, just as nurses know other nurses. Nourish the relationships you form so that prospective clients will remember you and stay in touch.

~ 95 ~

Many of my referrals have come from attorneys who have never used my services but have heard about me from colleagues. Regardless of an attorney's specialty, consider any new contact to be a potential source of referrals. Always show up with a smile, be diligent, follow the steps you've learned in this book over and over again, and watch your business grow.

SET YOUR GOALS AND KEEP YOUR EYE ON THE PRIZE

"I don't want to work on Christmas Day this year. I want to be home with my family".

What do *you* want out of your life this year? Not wanting to work on Christmas Day was my very first goal for getting started as an LNC. Even before I was married and had children, I knew I would want to be home with my future family on holidays. I wrote the above statement on a piece of paper and put in my wallet so I would never forget where I'd been and where I was determined to go.

Make a list of goals and look at it every day. Keep it somewhere you can see it, like your bathroom mirror or refrigerator door. Everything you have striven for and accomplished as a nurse has led you to the right place, at the right time. You're on the verge of becoming a legal nurse consultant during the industry's infancy. You have the potential to bring more value to your clients than you know. Don't think of your marketing efforts as selling. Think of them as opportunities to educate people about how amazing legal nurse consultants are.

Be proactive and don't let rejections slow you down. Rejection is simply part of being the boss, so never take it personally. This is business. You're

CRUSH IT: THE LEGAL NURSE BLUEPRINT FOR SUCCESS

going to hear "no" more often than "yes". In fact, start thinking about how you can use the word "no" to sharpen your pitch and keep going.

You've got this. You really do. I believe in you.

My life changed once I stopped acting out of fear and started following my dreams. Stay positive and remember that you're in this for the long haul. Success doesn't happen overnight. Every little action you complete towards your goals adds up to success. A little progress each day can build your business into a strong, profitable enterprise.

I always remember the 90-day rule: *whatever seeds you plant now will likely not come to fruition for at least ninety days. Your business is like a garden. It requires daily maintenance to bloom.*

So, no more excuses. Here's to our success! Come join us in the NNC lounge [https://www.nnc-members.com/become-a-nnc-member/] and let's get started.

I'm living the dream, and I want you to live yours.

Are you ready?

NOTES

NOTES

NOTES

Made in the USA
Columbia, SC
14 December 2019

If This Book Has Inspired You...

...or caused you to rethink the way you deliver customer service in your business, then it has accomplished its objective. By that, I am encouraged and fulfilled.

However, as with any productive consulting session or seminar you attend, this book may just be the beginning, inspiring new questions and revealing even more processes to be developed and tested on your journey toward improvement. What will you do differently when your next customer comes to your business? Remember, if nothing changes, it will remain the same.

The process of improving customer service starts today. If you find yourself in need of a more personalized consultation, or if you would like to bring the message of *Customer Service is a Contact Sport*™ to your retail organization via a seminar or customized workshop, contact Customer Service Solutions, Inc. at info@customerservicesolutions.com, or visit our website: www.customerservicesolutions.com.

I bid you well in your quest to improve the most important aspect of your business, your service to the customers who ultimately determine the success of your business.

Joseph Rosales, President
Customer Service Solutions, Inc.

Chapter Nine Summary
- Measure, measure, measure
- Sometimes you just need a little more effort
- Improve your game
- Work on being more consistent
- Be objective
- You don't know what you don't know
- Use the power of synergy